FREEDOM from BOSSES FOREVER

How to take control of your own destiny by going it alone

By Tony Robinson OBE
(with **Soculitherz**–pronounced So-cool-it-hurts)

If you choose to drink, eat, make love or cut your toenails whilst reading this book, please do this responsibly. Remember the value of your home can go up as well as down. Any personal details that you provide to Government may remain in the public domain.

This small, popular and highly acclaimed book on enterprise has an interesting history. This is an updated version of 'Stripping for Freedom' which was first published in June 2009 with a second edition published in January 2010 as softback and eBook. In late 2013 'Stripping for Freedom' was completely revised and improved as a brand new eBook entitled 'Freedom from Bosses Forever'.

The high sales and critical acclaim for 'Freedom from Bosses Forever' created the demand for the publishing of this softback version. The book has been Start Your Business Magazine's Editor's Book Choice of the Month and nominated for Small Business Book of the Year - 2014 in the 'Start Up' category.

Copyright © The Business Advisory Bureau Limited

ISBN 978-1-8491449-3-3

Published by: BAB, The Business Advisory Bureau Limited, Publications August 2014

This book is licensed for your personal enjoyment only. It may not be sold or given away to other people. If you would like to share this book with another person, then please purchase an additional copy for each person. You may not reproduce this work, in part or in its entirety, without the express written permission of the author.

Most of the characters in this book and the co-author, Soculitherz, are fictitious. Any resemblance to real persons, living or dead is purely co-incidental.

This book is dedicated to my best friend, business partner and editor of all my work since 1986, Clare Francis. It is written in awe of the late Miles Kington and PG Wodehouse who have given me a lifetime of laughter.

Other books by Tony Robinson OBE with Soculitherz are

'Buzzing with the Entrepreneurs' Jan 2004 ISBN 0 9512488 39

'Stripping for Freedom' Jan 2010 ISBN 978 0 9512488 43

Allegedly, other books by Leonora Soculitherz are

'The Edible Desire' (1995);

'Bong in the Orange Grove' (1997);

Over Strung and Under Nourished (2002)

What they've said about this book:

For your interest, here are some reader reviews of the original version of this book which was entitled 'Stripping for Freedom'.

2014 reader reviews of the eBook version of 'Freedom from Bosses Forever' can be found on Amazon and this book has a 5 star customer rating. Book critics' reviews can be found on the 'Freedom from Bosses Forever' Facebook page and at http://TonyRobinsonOBE.com

***

'I've discovered a rare treat. A business book that's valuable and very funny too.'

By Dave Sumner-Smith who is former editor/programme director of b2b business hub, Home Business Network and Telegraph Business Club

When is the last time you read a business book that made you laugh out loud? Every month there seems to be scores of new books about different aspects of business. But many of them seem to cover the same old ground. Very few focus on the special issues relating to running a business from home. And very, very few have ever made me laugh.

'Stripping for Freedom' is an exception to the rule. Written by the Canadian 'writer, broadcaster and celebrity' Leonora Soculitherz (no, I hadn't heard of her either), the book revolves around the basic principle that your business should be based on offering whatever you have got that is wanted by people with money. Even if that means you end up as a lap dancer (though doing that at home is unlikely to generate much revenue, I suspect!).

Written in a fun, bold style that you will either love or hate, it is peppered with 'Leonorisms' ("Leave your old company style behind you. You are now your own brand, so dress to impress") and other advice. When talking about 'Dealing with Regulations', for example, she advises that you should "be generally aware of the regulations around your own enterprise, but don't fall into the trap of trying to comply with it all. Comply only when you have to. Get this wrong and you'll find you're legal but bust, because you had no time or money left to start and run your business."

'Can I sue for emotional stress?!'

By Eva Davies who is Owner/Director, The Electric Zone Online retailer selling luxury electronics, intelligent gadgets and contemporary furniture

OK Tony I am most displeased with you and Clare – you shouldn't have written such a funny book.

Picture the scene – we are taking a family holiday in Brighton and I have found a good deal at The Grand Hotel (swanky or what)

One afternoon it is raining so I decide to have tea and a nice read in the lounge. I stupidly took Stripping for Freedom with me and firstly had raised eyebrows from the waiter. Secondly and worst – I started laughing aloud so hard that it came out as a snort – v. embarrassing – other guests lowered their copies of the Telegraph and Wisden to look disapprovingly at me!

Seriously it is so funny, Tony.

Do hope I get to meet you in the flesh in the future. Do you venture south – Londoners are quite friendly once you get over the language barrier

Have got to go and cut down my thick tights now – thank Leonora for the tip – us good Indian girls don't like to waste money!

'The funniest hard-hitting business book, that is absolutely full of business truth'

By Stefan Topfer who is Chairman and CEO WinWeb Global entrepreneur, cloud software and apps and Editor of The Small Business Blog

"Soculitherz has written books before, but this one is, in my opinion, the best she has ever written for anyone who wants to take control of their own destiny by going it alone. At the same time this is the funniest hard-hitting business book, that is absolutely full of business truth, I have ever read – some have called this book "whacky" and I can agree with that to some extent. Why else would I now deny to sitting her in winter at my home desk with my fleece on – heck, I even would deny owning a fleece.

Confused? Fasten your seat belt and read the book and find out why Zsa Zsa Gabor, "...wanted a man who only has to be kind and understanding. Is that too much to ask of a multi-millionaire?" Find out why this book is not only for women and why it is so relevant for you and your entrepreneurial endeavours.

Leonora, with the help of her "underwhelming" helper Tony Robinson, cuts through the chase, tells it how it is and then delivers the distilled business truth in a fashion that entertains as much as it is relevant.

"Stripping" for freedom paints a picture of brutally honest business acumen and asks you how much you really want it – and by getting you to strip your ambitions bare in the process of reading, this book leaves you in no doubt on who has to make it happen – You!

If you plan to read one book this holiday season, make it "Stripping for Freedom" – you will by mightily entertained with humorous insights, exposed yet practical business knowledge whilst being delighted and amused with the double meaning of words. I guess as you can tell, I loved this book,.... just don't tell her about the fleece – you must promise!"

'Well worth absorbing'

By Gail Purvies a writer who edits Compute Scotland in which this review appeared. Gail was also a friend from school days of the late Miles Kington, the brilliant humorous writer.

Ably assisted by Tony Robinson (who despite this, emerges as the fall guy) and judiciously edited by Clare Francis, author Leonora Soculitherz, takes her own ultra fashionably, chatty, confidential route through "Stripping for Freedom" or "taking control of your own destiny by going it alone" as an entrepreneur.

For lazy readers with an urge to get at the key issues, nothing is easier than page flicking for Leonorisms or 'truths" helpfully printed in easily seen bold lettering. The first one is core to the whole book. 'Think of a lap dancer: what have you got to offer that people with money to spend, want?'

Closely followed by "in a recession, don't just fish in the private sector pool for your customers because the public sector fish are fatter and easier to catch (especially between January to the end of March when they have got to get rid of all that's remaining of their budgets and allowances).

For a Scottish biased website, it's a pleasure to see good work being recognised. Leonora points out 'The Highlands and Islands of Scotland recognise the importance of providing consistently high levels of free training and support to start up and existing micro enterprise owners to ensure they have the same chance of success as in any other career.'

On essential effective networking the highlight is 'choose productive networks from which you can learn, gain a profile and be given and give referrals.'

But this idle approach will lose the humour, and some interesting and reflective stories, well worth absorbing. Take the chapter on Scarborough. Why Scarborough? Well it's hats off to Scarborough, which with a population of 50,000 first won "The Most Enterprising Place in Yorkshire,' then 'The Most Enterprising place in Britain,' to be ultimately crowned in Prague as, 'The Most Enterprising Town in Europe.' That Scarborough chapter has lots to teach any budding business owner.

The best Leonorism is of course the last, and concerns the daily topping up of the three pots. But you've got 183 pages to strip through first, by which time you should have worked out the three pot issue.

'Laughing Out Loud'

By Julie Stanford who is a designer, radio presenter and President of Brighton & Hove Chamber of Commerce. Julie developed, owns and publishes through Cobweb, the Essential Business Guide - the top UK reference guide for small business owners.

I'm really enjoying reading Stripping for Freedom' (indeed my snort of laughter woke up a few sleeping travellers on a Brighton to Victoria train when I read the part about looking good being simply a matter of how well you tuck in your bits!)

'An Essential Read'

By Dr Robert Murray who was formerly Enterprise Coordinator at Nottingham Trent University

Being retired, I read this book just for its humour. It certainly succeeded in that respect as the jokes and situations were to my liking. However, the important messages came across and I have spent the weeks since I read Leonora's thesis, telling my friends that the country is simply doing the wrong things.

Why do we spend tens of thousands of pounds to create one job in the big, high tech, industries when a few hundred would give the small entrepreneur the time to become established? Why don't we support small business and encourage the ideas that come from people of all ages?

Fantastic advice in the book and it does mean freedom to liberate people to accomplish a successful business that is their dream.

We need Leonora in a position of power to save us from the professional, blinkered politicians, particularly those who are in power from their titles rather than from the ballot box.

'Light style, serious message'

By George Derbyshire OBE who was Chief Executive of the National Federation of Enterprise Agencies

Books about entrepreneurship come in different styles, but usually all end up as lists. This one is different. Persevere: amidst the anecdotes and the quirky humour there is lots of serious guidance for new entrepreneurs. And some questions which ought to make one or two people in Whitehall shuffle on their seats in embarrassment. Why does nearly all the government money go to the usual suspects?

'Entertaining and informative'

By Anthony Haynes who is a Literary Agent, Publisher and Co-Owner of Higher & Professional

The framework of this book is a narrative told by a Canadian author (and style guru) exploring entrepreneurship (and the lack of support for micro-enterprises) in the UK. The structure makes the book both entertaining (I particularly liked the portrait of Jools, the businesswoman who ruins everyone's train journey by yelling into her mobile throughout the journey) and informative: there's good, down to earth, advice for people running, or intending to run, their own (genuinely) small businesses. And there are some good jokes too.

'Fancy a Leonorism…?'

By Nat Hardwick who is a Musician, IT Consultant and Director of the UK Sector Skills Body for Small Firms and Business Support – SFEDI Group

What a thoroughly enjoyable read…! By turns satirical, thought-provoking and darkly comic. Many a laugh-out-loud moment… Leonora takes us on a whistle stop tour de force of our own entrepreneurial culture and holds up a (wildly fashionable) mirror… but don't be surprised if you don't like all that you see!

Contact Details

Tony Robinson OBE Speaker & Author
http://TonyRobinsonOBE.com
Twitter: @TonyRobinsonOBE and on LinkedIn & Facebook & Pinterest & YouTube
E-mail: tony@EnterpriseRockers.co.uk

Enterprise Rockers Free & Indie, Global Community of micro business owners.
http://EnterpriseRockers.co.uk & http://EnterpriseRockers.com
Twitter: @EnterpriseRocks and Groups on LinkedIn & Facebook

Tony Robinson OBE & Soculitherz both write for
The Small Business Blog http://sme-blog.com
& recommend for great business cloud software & apps
http://WinWeb.com
Pinterest Soculitherz - Men's Fashion Faux Pas
http://pinterest.com/tonyrobinsonobe/men-s-fashion-faux-pas-by-leonora-soculitherz/

Cover Design by LoveYourCovers.com
Formatted by Writers Block Author Services

Contents

PROLOGUE by Tony Robinson OBE 1

Introduction
Handbags, Gladrags and K 3

Chapter One
Chunky Businesses 9

Chapter Two
Who Moved My Fleece? 21

Chapter Three
The Magic of Drinking Big 33

Chapter Four
In Search of Essence of Scarborough 42

Chapter Five
The Naked Reader 57

Chapter Six
How To Win Men and Affluent Friends 68

Chapter Seven
The 'M' myth 79

Chapter Eight
Small is cool 99

Chapter Nine
Lost In Translation 112

Chapter Ten
The Answer is Blowing in the Wind 121

Postscript 135

Useful websites 138

ABOUT THE AUTHORS of Freedom from Bosses Forever ... 141

A Final Piece of Fun? 144

FREEDOM from

BOSSES FOREVER

Tony Robinson OBE (with Soculitherz)

PROLOGUE by Tony Robinson OBE

This book is for anyone thinking of starting their own business. It is also for anyone that is interested in enterprise, whether their own or another's enterprise. Most of all it's perfect for anyone wanting to read a funny book on business, particularly those yearning to escape the corporate cubicle and be free from bosses forever.

The book was first published as 'Stripping for Freedom' by Leonora Soculitherz with me as co-author. I have updated it and removed any rude bits. I have added in many valuable, free to use, web links to help anyone succeed as their own boss.

Soculitherz (pronounced So-cool-it-hurts) has asked me to make it clear that she wants no part of 'Freedom from Bosses Forever', that this is a totally unauthorized publication and that I am an imbecile.

Since collaborating with me to write 'Stripping for Freedom', Canadian fashionista and investigative journalist, Ms Leonora Soculitherz is now known by the single name 'Soculitherz'. Many, equally famous, celebrities are known by single names, such as; Madonna, Cher, Beyonce, Rihanna and Batman.

It is not known whether Soculitherz will ever return to the UK to see me again or indeed to write another book on enterprise. I have had an e-mail from her which stated 'You are pathetic and I'm very unhappy about you massacring my book.

My latest erotic thriller, '50 Sheds du Lait' is about a fit French, billionaire, dairy farmer investigating the disappearance of big supermarket bosses. He's hooked on gorgonzola and addicted to early morning visits to the 'Beyond the Pail Room' with a trainee yoghurt maker.

Anyway, writing the 'ooh la la' first meeting of the stylish lady chief of police with the farmer, with the fabulous six pack, reminds me how unfortunate I've been to ever meet you - my hapless, hopeless and sadly dressed excuse for an agent.'

FREEDOM from BOSSES FOREVER

I think Soculitherz is interested in other things. So, ladies and gentlemen, I proudly present 'Freedom from Bosses Forever', formerly 'Stripping for Freedom'. It begins with Soculitherz explaining where she got the idea for the title of the original book.

Tony Robinson OBE (with Soculitherz)

Introduction

Handbags, Gladrags and K

One of the perils of being accessible as a writer, broadcaster and celebrity is that everyone thinks they have the right to interrupt me in mid flow (of writing this book). Other celebrities, particularly, seem to think they have the right to seek my advice at any time. I'd better deal with them before I continue this introduction.

So, Delia from Norwich, never use bagged lettuce as it's washed in a chlorine solution twenty times more concentrated than in your swimming pool. Also, however exciting the team win is, never ever jump in the bath with seventeen footballers – again.

Kate from Croydon, you're wonderful but I still need to give you a layering master class and, No, you're not too old now to have a freebie Paddington Chloe handbag, but although oversized, slouchy shapes are still good in handbags, (they make you look even thinner), they remain most uncool in boyfriends.

As for Fay in the West Country, I'm sorry to say I haven't got a definitive feminist reaction to your views yet. I've sent texts to my girlfriends to poll them on whether a) they think it is right to fake orgasms for the man's benefit and b) sex can also be great without an orgasm.

However, from their limited response to date, I think we must assume that food, clothes, shoes and a good night's sleep are the issues currently closer to their hearts. One said that for a man 'who could listen', it might be worth the pretence in a), but most thought that such a man will never exist. Another said that 'men who hate women can be great lovers', so work all that stuff out.

Also, in one case 'giving up Twix chocolate bars would be tougher than giving up sex with any man', which I suppose could answer a) and b). I did try to get a male view and sent a text to my Canadian

FREEDOM from BOSSES FOREVER

soul mate and leading life coach, Rock Heathcliff, and below is our repartee:

'Me: a fave UK author & feminist says it's OK for wmn 2 fake orgasm 2 keep the relationship sweet – do u agree?

Rock: Don't get it!!

Me: Reason u don't get it is cos the rabbit does it better.

Rock: Wot??

Me: Forget it.'

Anyway, back to the flow. I've been asked countless times whether I know anything about stripping from personal experience, as per my alluring title for this book. The answer is 'something'.

Before I arrived in England to write this book I learned a little about stripping for a living from my new friend K (short for Kylie). Using my publisher's paltry advance, I asked K to spend a week with me in Malta to tell me about her life and the people she meets.

K was recommended to me by my very best English friend Michaela, (Mickey), whom you'll meet later in the book. I'd asked Mickey if she knew anyone who was successful as a stripper or table dancer. It had to be someone who worked at one of the top London clubs where the cream of the UK's financial sector spent their time relaxing or entertaining clients after a hard day spent gambling away the UK economy.

K seems a bit like the Natalie Portman character in the film 'Closer'. She claims she is all powerful in front of drunken businessmen at what she calls a 'classy' table side dancing club. I've been there since and the furnishings are a bit like the clientele – arrogant (perhaps a good new brand name for interior furnishings?), thick, rich and mostly in the dark.

K has a body to die for. Literally, for there is anguish on many of the punters' faces as they consider whether it is worth breaching the 'no touching' rule and dying from a five gorilla mauling as they are ejected.

Every move is monitored on camera, so it appears a safe environment for the seductive, sensuous and certainly sickeningly slim K. (Did you know that two thirds of the CCTV cameras manufactured worldwide end up in the UK and the UK government is revered as being the best at devising ways of collecting data on all of its citizens? Comforting for K.)

Fortunately for the heavily protected K she only has to say 'thank you' for the bundles of notes that are thrust her way, for her voice is not her greatest asset. Whilst she wants to sound sultry like Norah Jones, I'm afraid that it comes out like Cyndi Lauper on speed. Does that sound a bit catty?

K is independent and, in her own way, an entrepreneur. She takes controlled risks in doing something in a special way that will make her money. Her body is her freedom. K wasn't very forthcoming about what goes on in the private rooms – the 'champagne rooms – where the big money is. Here, Cristal-sodden, testosterone fuelled traders, accountants and lawyers, hyped up by their big wins or big losses in the City, will exchange £thousands in return for K's personal attention.

All K would say on the subject of the private dances, or even whether she'd meet a client outside the club, was 'we have power, we have protection, we can do numb and dumb... and thinking of the money certainly helps'.

After uni. and a post grad. Comms. course, K joined a large PR agency in London, where she met Mickey. Within eighteen months she was sick of the corporate lifestyle and the free meals and drinks, which were also making her fat. K worked out the fastest way of making great money in order to do with it what she wanted to please herself.

FREEDOM from BOSSES FOREVER

K *strips* for freedom, but anyone without a job, stuck in a boring job or just sickened by the rat race or public institutions can also choose, (not literally), to do this. My book will show you how and why you should too.

Through my interviews I identify many valuable and unassailable truths. These truths are called Leonorisms and give you guidance. **Leonorisms** appear in bold. There are really lots of them throughout this book. The first one, related to K, which you can consider, dear reader, is:

1. Think of a lap dancer: what have you got to offer that people with money to spend, want?'

In order to learn about K, I persuaded her to leave winter in London for a week and head for the sun in Malta. What a disaster! The idea of topping up the tans for a week was a good one, but I hadn't realized how focused K is on remaining absolutely blemish free. I guess if you're willing to go to the torture chamber regularly for a Brazilian or Hollywood, then you're unlikely to be someone who allows environmental hazards like sun and insects to mess with the way you want to look.

The holiday started badly as the chlorinated water from our evening swim in the hotel pool led to an unfortunate streaking of K's massively costly, fake St Tropez tan.

K is obsessive about her body. That extends to working out every day for between 2 and 4 hours, yet she does everything outside covered up from head to toe. For example, at 7 a.m. she'd be power walking along Sliema promenade to St Julian and back, along with hundreds of others.

No-one would be able to pick her out and no-one would guess sex, age, ethnicity or angst as she is swathed in track suit, hoodie over baseball hat, sunglasses and earphones. She looked ready for an uprising in Athens, but these are the lengths to which she will go to remain blemish free.

Tony Robinson OBE (with Soculitherz)

I spend my life ensuring I always look naturally gorgeous, but with nothing like the tenacity of K. Nevertheless, her reluctance to expose her skin to the elements does seem a tad crazy for someone who wouldn't think twice about risking all under the surgeon's knife, to enhance her looks. Injections from knitting needle sized hypodermics is also par for her silken course. Botox is a six monthly routine and she was one of the first to have a Macrolane injection to get bigger breasts. This, too, will require a top up in a year or so.

Any type of body invasion from nature itself is not on K's agenda. Water sports are clearly out. Equally, she reckons that walking outside with skin exposed during the day, carries a 40% chance of a graze, cut or bruise, and in the evening there is the unacceptable 60% chance of an insect bite. K even looked distinctly uncomfortable at breakfast at the Park Hotel. I guessed that she was wondering if the silver hair, age spots or the many ailments being exhibited by the residents, could be passed on through the self service spoons for the baked beans and scrambled eggs.

Every biting bug in the region must have passed the word that K's skin was a 'not to be missed' delicacy and the opportunity for a gourmet feast for all Maltese flying insects. After a while I was convinced that an advance scouting party of wasps was sent to establish the exact venue for the banquet. Once they got a whiff of 'K's No7', they would hover above her, buzzing loudly. Within minutes, bugs of all manner and classes, well dressed for dinner, would join the scouts looking to nibble away merrily.

The bugs were only one of many hazards to the body beautiful. To K, the only way to be exposed to the sun is for each body part to receive exactly the same amount of exposure. Tanning herself is therefore a very precise, very time consuming and very boring business. I was interested though that the book she was reading, given to her by one of her regular clients from the City, was one of mine – 'Bong in the Orange Grove'. At least the woman has taste; but frankly, by the end of the week I'd happily have left her turning on a roasting spit.

FREEDOM from BOSSES FOREVER

Don't get me wrong: I admire loads about K. It's just that her obsession with 'blemish free', seemed to be getting in the way of our opportunity to enjoy the historic sights of Malta. I also got fed up with always trying to remain 'front on' when next to her and never walking in front of her either, so that the subject of comparative bum sizes would never come up.

There are two Leonorisms K said to me over the course of the week, which I need to pass on to you if you're thinking of going it alone:

"My work is something that I know many other women find repulsive.

2. Friends, family or professional advisers may not approve, but don't let them get in the way. If you want it, go and get it" and;

3. Few are willing to pay the price in terms of hard work and lost friends in order to achieve their aims".

K is only one of the many experts, in many different locations, including London, Madrid, New York, Toronto and Scarborough whom I've used to help me explain how anyone and everyone can escape the rat race and go it alone by stripping for freedom. I've ensured that you won't have heard of most of these experts. However, K is the only one who always succeeds with the skinny jeans day-into-evening solution. So what?

Tony Robinson OBE (with Soculitherz)

Chapter One

Chunky Businesses

It is very vulgar to talk about one's own business. Only stockbrokers do that, and then merely at dinner parties

Oscar Wilde
The Importance of Being Earnest, Act 3 (1895)

Call me Leonora, not Leo, Lee, Lenny or any man's name. There are very few true celebrities around today. Regrettably, just five minutes on a reality TV show or being married to a sportsman can jerk you up the party invitation lists and into star studded events. This inevitably leads to these nouveau 'celebs.' being photographed in flagrante, which keeps them in the media gaze for a while longer than they deserve.

True celebrity is knowing what to wear, what to wear under it (i.e. spanx knickers – slim cognito mid thigh shaper), who to be with, when and where to arrive, what not to eat and drink, when to botox, what to speak against, what to support, how much to give to whom and when and, most of all, how to preserve your brand and name when everyone wants to shorten, familiarise or generally mess with it. So it is Gwyneth, Victoria, Nicole, Jennifer and Leonora – in full!

As a Canadian I may for just a millisecond put up with being called American, but I will not tolerate what I call 'chumminess'. Only my friends and family and perhaps my celebrity stalker, who e-mails me the sweetest things, are allowed to tease me about the lengths I'll go to enhance my public persona. If highlights, extensions, affairs or even icing my nipples;

4. Makes me stand out from the crowd, then it is not only my business, it is only me doing business.

5. I succeed because of who I have made myself into. You can succeed in the way you want too.

Through over eighty **Leonorisms** in this book I will show you how you can be free from bosses forever by going it alone in business of your own. So, leave the rat race behind. Never again be subject to the torture and degradation of performance appraisals, away days, corporate training, helicopter visioning, bonding and brainstorming.

Never again have to pretend to smile or encourage your boss through one cringe-worthy speech after another at company events like birthdays, someone starting, leaving, dying or bringing in their new baby. No one really cares about these 'events' and no one really cares about you in your cubicle in big organisation hell. So, read on if you really want to control your own destiny by going it alone.

My story is already well known, but certainly when my spineless, unfaithful, cellist husband Gerard patronised me in public and on television I could have receded from view forever or, as I did, stuck a bow for posterity and my notoriety. No pain – no gain. His pain and my gain. I have the 'going it alone' T shirt.

I'd just been on vacation to the Shuswap, spending a week on a houseboat, when my publisher called and invited me to lunch at the Four Seasons Hotel in Toronto. Here he suggested to me that I should return to the recession ravished UK (the rest of the world is so happy about the US-UK special relationship, especially the financial sectors) to write a follow up to my 2004 best seller, '*Buzzing with the Entrepreneurs*'.

I sort of jumped at the chance. Only 'sort of', because although I felt eminently qualified for the assignment, it meant leaving Canada again and relearning the funny ways and expressions of the English. It would mean goodbye to gas, sidewalks, traffic circles, fries and

Leonard Cohen and hello to petrol, pavements, roundabouts, chips and Will Young.

There were four good reasons to be interested. Firstly, I'm always interested in trends that make money and make you famous and I'm sure that helping people become self employed, many of whom now have no viable alternative, coupled with solving a major UK political mystery, will do just that.

Secondly, I am more popular in the UK than in Canada – Dame Edna probably has the same problem in Australia – because of my weekly column.

Thirdly, I'm the best interviewer in the UK after 'Parky', and therefore the writer most likely to capture the real essence of entrepreneurship, the special juices needed for self employment.

Fourthly, I consider myself an entrepreneur – someone who has successfully 'stripped for freedom' – so I can separate the useful from the useless, the wheat from the chavs and the meat from the bullshit.

In short then, there is no better saviour to come to the bankrupt UK and set free those sad, manacled employees incarcerated in their 'open office' cubicles. I, Leonora Soculitherz, hear their screams for help, understand the despair in their corporate gibberish, and I must and will show them how to go it alone.

Of course, everything I have found out from the UK will work in other nations too. For example, the US desperately needs the Soculitherz treatment. It has a new and inspirational President, sure, but it's likely that many of their economic problems will only be solved by the next generation of entrepreneurs. Time and life march inexorably on and the decision to 'go it alone' now may be very right wherever you are in the world.

For example, co-pilots Sully (Sullenberg) and Skiles, the three cabin crew and the traffic controller who between them safely landed

FREEDOM from BOSSES FOREVER

Flight 1549 and all its passengers in the Hudson river, had 177 years between them of loyal, corporate aviation experience, but sadly felt that it counted for zip with their employers.

It was understandable that every leading US politician waxed lyrical about their heroism and the US Senate safety committee formally recognised that experienced personnel were the most important safety factor on Flight 1549. It was enlightening though that the crew took their one big worldwide TV opportunity to make sure we knew they weren't over impressed with the glory.

They made it clear that before the bird strike made them heroes and heroines, they'd taken 40% pay cuts, lost most of their pensions, taken second jobs, were working 7 days a week and didn't know a single person who wanted their jobs. So much for expecting Corporate America to look after their valued employees.

Brothers and sisters, it's time to do it for ourselves. The more of us who do it and are vocal about it, the more chance we have of getting our respective Governments to redistribute to us some of the finance, support and opportunities that currently go to the Corporates and institutions.

6. 'Stripping for freedom' means divesting yourself of everyone and everything that will get in the way of you controlling your own entrepreneurial destiny.

I have bared my body, my soul, my intellect and my charisma. The economic litmus test is that everything I supply my public, they buy in buckets-full. Reader, I don't want to prejudice your early conclusions from this authoritative work, but

7. I believe a supportive environment and family help a great deal in giving people the 'bottle' (as you English call it) to go it alone.

Tony Robinson OBE (with Soculitherz)

I lived my early years in Hull, close to Ottawa, in Canada, and our house was called 'The Parsonage'. It was up a steep road, separated from the other houses, and it overlooked a grim churchyard.

In truth, it was a greyish place, surrounded by bleak, undulating moorland, with just eight bare rooms and a stone staircase. Yet I remember how we three sisters, with our genius older brother, created light, colour, beauty and a fantasy world out of sand, water, blu-tack, paper clips and sweet wrappers. We weren't allowed glue because of my brother Grayson's tendency to sniff it.

The four of us would each take a side of the sand pit, with me directly opposite Grayson. The sandpit would represent far off and foreign lands populated by little colourful people whom we'd make out of the paperclips, blu-tack and sweet wrappers. Looking back, this is probably where I first gained my eye for fashion.

I would be Queen Antonia The Reasonable. Grayson would be King George, The Junior. Together we ruled the kingdom of Gundoil, where all the Gundoilers did as we said. My sisters were the Grand Protectors of the Funny Foreign Lands and they had to avoid provoking Gundoil into attacking and annexing their lands.

The fantasy was played out in silence, so that no-one could hear our plans or suspect our duplicity. We did this by tiny writing, often in heroic verse, on the sweet wrappers and making them into little aeroplanes which we flew across the sandpit to our partner in crime. We did think about publishing the contents of all these sweet wrappers to show off our brilliance to the world, but unfortunately Grayson had a nasty streak. When he took a dislike to anything he didn't understand in the game, he would just throw a bucket of water over everything. Eventually, we three sisters got fed up with rebuilding our worlds and anyway, we were getting really fat from eating all the sweets.

I didn't get my creativity and self belief from an 'unleash the creative tiger within' corporate training course involving climbing on and holding hands with my work colleagues so that my boss can climb to the top of the pyramid. No, I gave full rein to my creativity from an early age and I encourage all British parents to do the same for their children.

I digress. My Canadian publisher recognised the time was right for me to build on my earlier UK book called 'Buzzing with the Entrepreneurs'. He saw I had a role to play in solving an enduring political and economic mystery. He saw the need for me to provide genuine help to enable people to leave the rat race behind. He saw that my profile in the UK has never been higher. This was all pretty observant, since normally all he could see was my cleavage.

His exact briefing to me was "meet as many self employed folk and entrepreneurs as you can and report their practical success secrets, thus developing 'go it alone' guidance for all those who are considering leaving, or have left their jobs. Explain how they will need to strip for freedom. While you're at it, try and solve the big mystery that is baffling most of us about the UK. This is; 'Why are government ministers, senior civil servants, government advisers, failed bank chiefs and other major corporate and public sector CEOs getting very very rich whilst everything they touch is going bust?'

As he said these words my mobile played 'Je ne regrette rien'. At the other end was my fifth and hottest reason for going back to the UK, none other than the global phenomenon, motivational guru Ant Cracie, who was doing one of his firewalking tours in the UK;

'Hi Anty Panty. What's up?'

'Are you coming over to the UK soon?'

'Looks like it. In about three weeks time. To do a book on going it alone in the UK recession – what do you think?'

'Cool babe. I'll be in the UK for another six weeks so we can hook up.'

'What're you doing now?'

Tony Robinson OBE (with Soculitherz)

'In the bath singing 'Mercy' by Duffy, one of my all time fave songs.'

'Don't know it Ant, you must let me hear it sometime.'

'Sure babe... well, I have a bath most nights.

Look I was ringing because I just did a big gig for the Tochen network at the Crucible in Sheffield and you'll never guess what I found out?'

'Go on.'

'Your book *Bong in the Orange Grove* is one of the texts they quote from to train their members.'

'Nice – but who are the Tochen network?'

'Big in the UK, US, Japan and China. Founded by HR Tochen, in the late 1980s, you know... he also relaunched the christocratic movement. Anyway, they love you. When you're over I can get you to speak to them – big bucks'. See ya babe.

'Au revoir Anty.'

Even without Ant's endorsement you'll have realised by now I was going to take on this assignment. This was despite my knowledge of a major downside which I have not yet revealed to you.

This major downside was that my guide and mentor for this assignment would again be one Tony Robinson. This is not the famous 'Baldrick' actor and television presenter who digs up your ancestors, but a sorry looking substitute who is very proud to have been awarded an OBE for services to small firms and training. I'm sure that the Queen must have got the invitations to the Chelsea Flower Show and New Year's Honours list mixed up between the two Tony Robinsons.

FREEDOM from BOSSES FOREVER

I knew why I'd been assigned the talentless one of the two: my publisher could and will be paying him peanuts. He'll have accepted this offer with alacrity and gross obsequiousness, as he's lucky to get any work and is clearly always broke. No-one would dress that badly by design. How do you work with someone who says his greatest achievement is to have been with 600,000 others watching Hendrix, the Who, Free, Leonard Cohen, John B Sebastian, Taste, Joni Mitchell and others over 5 days at the Isle of Wight in 1970? It's as though his life is a freeze frame.

My publisher unsuccessfully tried to reassure me that the badly bearded one was still regarded as an expert on all things to do with self employment and he teased me into believing that TR had a few leads which might help in the second part of my assignment.

As my 'Buzzing' readers will know, I am just totally underwhelmed when Tony Robinson is ever in my presence. I have learned, however, that if he is going to be around, then I am best to bring an interpreter with me and wear waterproofs.

Understanding his pronunciation is a nightmare: it's not a great start when he introduces himself as 'Turnie Robbins'.

8. My advice is never to work with someone who can't pronounce their own name.

All similarly written words sound the same. For example, you have to guess whether 'her' is her, hare or hair and 'fur' is fur, fare or fair. A recurring phrase he used to use, which took me six months before I guessed the correct meaning, was 'kurching ancheesy girls'. This, I finally twigged, meant 'coaching and achieving goals'.

His co-ordination is even worse than his diction. You'll remember that my first introduction to him at a BAB/Entrepreneurs UK Awards' ceremony, saw him trip over his briefcase and throw his glass of wine over me. After wiping myself down I was exposed for over an hour to his unique ability to mispronounce most of the English language, whilst, from time to time, throwing more wine or canapés over me. This is because he gesticulates to make each incomprehensible point, forgetting that he has both hands full of refreshments.

Any room he's in where networking is going on resembles a battlefield. Some of the effect is caused by the sorry state of furnishings and clothes as a result of the flying foodstuffs, but many women in the room will also look distinctly the worse for wear, due, not to drink but to TR's lack of co-ordination.

TR has never got the hang of the two cheek/kiss greeting with the opposite sex. In the best of cases this just leads to the woman sporting an ugly red rash from his beard for an hour or so, but in the worst of cases it leads to a cracked head, black eye or broken nose.

Anyway, enough of TR. You'll meet him soon, as I intend to travel by train directly from Manchester airport to Scarborough, where he lives, to sort out who does what on my assignment.

I'm writing this on the Air Malta plane to Manchester. Interestingly it is an all male cabin crew. Cool – I wonder if they've got a woman pilot? One of the things I did before leaving Canada for Malta was to contact a few of the entrepreneurs to whom I'd spoken previously when I did 'Buzzing' in '04. I wanted to find out just what effect the recession was having on small and home business owners in the UK. Top of my contacts list were Ethel and Ernie Brigstock in Brighton, who co-own a small chain of fish and chip café shops on the south coast.

When I last spoke to them, both their 'Cod is Cool' establishments were doing well and this was in no small part due to the image and brand Ethel and Ernie had created. Back in the day, the Brigstocks recognised that to fulfil their expansion plans they'd need to shape up; not just in a business sense, but personally too.

Between them, in just six months, they lost a whopping sixty-eight pounds, using the Flatkin food combining diet. This allowed them and their staff to wear their new, corporate, French-style uniforms

FREEDOM from BOSSES FOREVER

with pride. It was Ethel – then 49 and a petite and newly slimline 180 lbs – who was credited with coming up with the 'Cod is Cool' restaurant concept.

When I interviewed her she said: "We've always led by example in this sector, often punching above our weight. We were the first café-shops to copy the idea of putting fish and chip bags on a circular conveyor belt, in the style of 'Yo Sushi!' restaurants. Our café-shops look swish and welcoming in their new, modern, red, orange and blue colours, but what's the point of them looking good if we look like buckets of lard?"

I was impressed and remember even trying the Flatkin diet, but it was easier for them as they had the high quantities of potatoes needed for it and I didn't. They were clearly trend setters though. Any fish and chip shop proprietors who can create an establishment that gets the English to buy a bottle of wine with their fish and chips rather than the usual cup of tea, (with bread and butter) have to be very special entrepreneurs.

Anyway, when I rang them it was Ernie who answered the phone. After exchanging pleasantries I asked him: 'how is the UK recession affecting your business?'.

E: It's tough. We're still getting the visitors, especially in Brighton, because of the conference trade, but they're just not spending as much. I think the hotels and the B&Bs will just about be OK for the season as the exchange rate is so bad for Brits going abroad, but cafés, restaurants and pubs will struggle.

L: So you wouldn't advise people to go it alone in their own business at the moment?

E: Not saying that. Just saying it's a tough business environment, which means you've got to be even smarter to survive and thrive.

L: So what are you doing?

E: Well, we've had to completely re-brand, – not the food type, interiors or the basic image – what we're known for. Even the name of the cafés has had to change. We've had to attract a new type of customer all over again.

L: Sounds expensive Ernie. I thought a brand was for life?

E: Bugger that, Leonora, 'scuse my French. It was expensive, but we felt that we needed to go in the opposite direction from the rest of the fish and chip shop sector in order to attract the clientele who have the money to spend and are willing to spend it with us, even though our prices would be the highest.

L: Is it working? I can't begin to guess what you've done?

E: It was simple really. There's been a big media outcry over here over the organised abuse of expense allowances that MPs, MEPs, civil servants and others get. As you know, we always did really well out of local councillors and their guests at our 'Cod is Cool' shops. Ethel said one day 'We could be the answer to their problems. We're licensed, so they can have good wine and no-one will criticise them for spending their allowances on traditional fish and chips. We just need a reason why they should come to us rather than anyone else.

L: And?

E: And that's when I read about some of these super chefs who appear on the telly banging on about not eating cod and other fish we sell because it was overfished. 'Unsustainable', that's the word, meaning you can't plant a fish like you can a tree once you've killed it.

L: So?

E: So, we now only sell fish, (still in our patent beery batter), which isn't overfished such as dab, flounder, megrim sole, grey mullet, gurnard and pollack – mainly pollack. There's no-one else doing it and we can charge higher prices. In fact, we've renamed our cafés

FREEDOM from BOSSES FOREVER

'Sustainably the Best' with the slogan 'We're the Dog's Pollack'. A bit long, but it gets the message across. Now the councillors, MEPs, MPs, civil servants and their guests come along with a clear conscience to our unique but traditional seaside eating experience, to be relieved of their onerous expense allowances. Brilliant eh?

I had to admit it was brilliant. In fact, before we touch down at Manchester airport I'll leave all you potential strippers for freedom with a Leonorism that springs to mind from this chat with Ernie Brigstock.

9. In a recession don't just fish in the private sector pool for your customers, because the public sector fish are fatter and easier to catch (especially at the end of their budget year when they have to get rid of all that's left).

Tony Robinson OBE (with Soculitherz)

Chapter Two

Who Moved My Fleece?

Clothes make the man. Naked people have little or no influence in society.

Mark Twain
More Maxims of Mark Twain ed. Mark Johnson (1927)

I'll deal right now with those of you who are curious about what Oakley shades I wear (and generally just what not to wear anywhere). They're Oakley Razrwire (that is spelt correctly, as is Bluetooth – which they have) in pewter/ black, of course. Oh and stay clear of frosted lipstick, black leather, anything tight, acid colours, pale leggings, girlie frills and animal prints. Ankle boots can still be cool, but with leggings means pigs' trotters. OK?

Arriving at Manchester airport, you can't help but be struck by the lack of attention to clothes and body image in England. It looks like fleece city. This is good news for me, because reading my weekly column about what's hot and what's not in style and people, (and in my younger days about the dating scene too), must seem like another world to most Brits.

Thankfully for me, my readership figures indicate that my world must interest them. It gives me a mission in life too and if anyone is capable of changing the British style culture it is me, Leonora Soculitherz.

I sometimes think I must be part of the same UK phenomenon as the massive industry producing fitness DVDs that top all the retail charts. Millions of Brits must sit in their armchairs, in their fleeces, snacking on Cheerios, cheese on toast or BLTs watching these DVDs, with no intention of doing any of the exercises.

FREEDOM from BOSSES FOREVER

Perhaps I should bring out an exercise DVD based on getting fit through exercises related to watching the DVD from your armchair. It could include tensing abdomen and arm muscles as you remove your fleece, stretching between snack mouthfuls, using the remote as a dumbbell, rolling your head, winking (winking – Anty!) and so on.

Anyway, the point here, dear reader, is that I absolutely will not allow you to use this book in the same way as the constantly seated and fleeced use fitness DVDs. I will use all my skills as an investigative journalist to uncover words of wisdom from entrepreneurs that will enable you to go it alone successfully. At the very least, I command you to put my tips into practice.

I'm now writing this in the allegedly first class carriage of the allegedly trans-pennine express between Manchester airport and Scarborough. I use the word 'allegedly', as this train does neither 'first class' (just room enough to swing the proverbial cat) nor 'express'. Neither does it have a Wi-Fi internet connection, which frustratingly means that by the time I get to Scarborough, Stephen Fry will already be 200 tweets in the day ahead of me on Twitter.

I notice that your Government is just advertising for a Director to join the Civil Service, responsible for promoting Government on web/social networking sites. (Nom de Dieu! is every senior job in your Civil Service above £120k salary?). I'd have thought that instead of advertising, they could have a tweet out between Jonathan Ross and Stephen Fry.

Why isn't it really first class? The Northern train guards feel so sorry for the exorbitant prices paid by economy class passengers, with or without concessions, that when we get to Manchester Piccadilly, they let the world and his dog and screaming kids with tomato ketchup slavering down their chins from their Burger King Whoppa Deal, into the first class area. It's no good me complaining, as I can't understand a word of what they say in response to my complaint.

Anyway, when the rabble arrives I'll be safely secured in a corner seat, with a barricade made out of my cases. This will protect me and

Tony Robinson OBE (with Soculitherz)

my laptop from said kids lobbing empty drink cartons back over their heads at me, said mums falling off their wedges onto me, and businessmen squirting milk over me as they struggle to open those little plastic tubs for their coffee.

Before I get to Scarborough I'll use the next two chapters to update you on everything I've learned in readiness for my latest little sojourn and assignment in the UK. There are two, interlinked but unique features of this book that will enhance your reading experience.

Firstly, in this chapter, I'll explain why most of the tips I give you will come from interviews with entrepreneurs of whom, I promise you, you will not have heard. This is despite the fact that I'm known and admired by many of the UK's leading and celebrity entrepreneurs and currently in a steamy relationship with the hunkiest of all American entrepreneurs, Ant Cracie.

From my knowledge of them, I'll describe to you some of the limitations of following the counsel of these celebrity entrepreneurs. Fear not: I will still provide you with Leonorisms from this knowledge, which will help you to go it alone.

Secondly, in the next chapter, I'll explain why my publisher and other influential Brits feel that whilst I successfully solved the management gurus' murders, which I recorded in "Buzzing with the Entrepreneurs" in 2004, this was the beginning, not the end of the much bigger story.

Regular readers will remember that the UK press wittily called it a hunt for a 'cereal killer', because the perpetrators frequently disrupted and ruined leadership and management gurus' speeches at breakfast seminars. Although I eventually uncovered the 'cereal killer', many of my correspondents suspect that it is likely that I only uncovered the tip of a much bigger, malevolent political, economic and criminal iceberg. I'll let you know what I've found out to date.

You've bought this book, probably at a knock down price (my publisher has no scruples), in order to learn from people who have

FREEDOM from BOSSES FOREVER

got the T shirt about how to go it alone successfully. You'll be in good company. Let's take the UK as an example. One in seven of the adult workforce is starting or running their own enterprise. Out of the 4.5 million business owner run enterprises with fewer than 10 employees, over half are home based and over 3 million have no employees.

Despite a recession, the number of self employed and proportion of all small enterprises in the UK run by their owner (currently 98% of all UK businesses) will continue to increase. There are a million more self employed and micro enterprise owners than there were last time the UK was in recession. Most earn less than £20k a year and work more than a 50 hour week. At least 40% of those starting their own enterprise see no better alternative for earning their living.

Small and home business owners are the new working class, but unfortunately these 6 million individuals have no single point of representation to UK government ministers and are therefore easily ignored. Yet very many countries, such as Canada (mine), New Zealand, Thailand, even Malta where I've just been, and closer to your home the Highlands and Islands of Scotland, recognise the importance of providing consistently high levels of free training and support to start up and existing micro enterprise owners, to ensure they have the same chance of success as in any other career.

So why does Leonora Soculitherz want you, as a general rule, to learn from entrepreneurs who are neither on the telly, speaking in stadia, nor advising Government? The answer is in the word 'authentic'; Leonora says:

10. "Go for what is 'real and now', not for what is 'reality and then'".

Let me explain. Sometimes I think that despite my huge intellect and striking looks my main role is just as a cataloguer of information. People information is often the most spellbinding. In a restaurant I'm never at my table, always everyone else's. I get information about your society from just watching.

Some of the information I bring you I've digested, filtered and polished from my fellow hacks in the media, but probably the very best information I'll provide you comes from my own interviews. I'm sure that living outside your country helps give me an objectivity about what's happening inside it and what information will help to release you from your 'commute to cubicle' work life in the UK.

For example, I read the other day that your Brit, ex Prime Minister, Tony Blair, regards himself as a small business owner now and "he's loving it". Should Leonora, therefore, interview him on your behalf for this book?

Tony Blair has over 20 staff, including some tall, slim, well suited, young men and probably a £30 million turnover. Both the staff and earnings appeared to be almost immediate acquisitions on leaving office.

He got a £5 million advance for his memoirs while drawing a £1.9 million salary as part time adviser to investment bank JP Morgan Chase and £1.5 million salary for advising Zurich Financial services. In addition he receives a healthy pension from his nearly 10 years in office and, of course, an allowance to run a private office. Of course more very big money comes from the top tier speaking circuit on which both he and his wife feature.

Most recently he has formed Tony Blair Associates, which is a commercial partnership 'to provide... strategic advice on both a commercial and pro-bono basis, on political trends and government reform'. Looking at the UK that he and Gordon Brown have created between them, it's rather a surprise that showing others how to create something similar is so lucrative! Should the Brits be proud or peeved that he is one of the world's highest paid consultants?

Dear reader, I know that seeing your ex-Prime Minister as a small business owner will have you crying tears of joy into your lunch box at the next big Institute of Directors' conference at the Albert Hall. He will be charming, entertaining, motivating and doubtless inspirational. However, and here you have to trust Leonora, he will be of absolutely no use to you earning your beans as a self employed person in the real world.

You also need to be careful – not as careful perhaps as with Mr Blair – in taking the advice of the many entrepreneur celebrities made by your reality television. The celeb. entrepreneurs in Dragons' Den for example, are certainly true entrepreneurs and worthy of great respect, but they're not necessarily as useful to you now as they would have been on their way up, before telly, before recognition, before being smoothed down and swallowing the corporate management and leadership dictionary.

Lord 'Suralan' Sugar is an interesting one. He does the equivalent 'hire and fire' role as Donald Trump in the UK version of 'The Apprentice'. TV makes him out to be a bully, yet he seems to have a very loyal and longstanding team. Those who have worked for him or contracted to him, including TR, regard him as practical, knowledgeable, funny and fair. Certainly the skills and know how he says are needed by you as a potential entrepreneur are absolutely spot on, as is his healthy scepticism on the value of most consultants.

Seems to me that he shouldn't just be Lord Alan, Enterprise Tsar, but he should be the Prime Minister. He could appoint a cabinet full of entrepreneurs. All the cabinet would then have the advantage of knowing the value of a pound(£). This helps when spending taxpayers' money. Your current political leaders do not live in the real world.

So they're good, but the people you won't have heard of whom I'll interview for you in this book, are better for you. Advice from well known entrepreneurs who now advise government officials carry exactly the same 'health warning'. It's amazing how quickly entrepreneurs can change their approach as they get used to the company of senior civil servants and government ministers. Is it planned?

They get to enjoy the hospitality, the history, the formality, the protocol, the jargon, the acronyms and the company. They then learn how to work with, rather than against, existing government policy and programmes and are eventually used to frame new policy and programmes in the areas Government wants them to.

So, don't necessarily believe that entrepreneurs who are wealthy, well connected, speak well, are in the public eye and have public and government approval are always your best guides to how to become self employed. There's a Leonorism in all this:

11. Most successful entrepreneurs do a lot of work for free, in order to get themselves into networks that contain money and influence.

Another group from whom it is wise to be cautious of taking advice is that of the personal and business development gurus. This is despite the fact that I almost lick the page of every book they write and like nothing better than a bit of rumpty in the sack with one of the most famous of them. Why then?

The seldom broadcast fact is that: 'the essence of what works in running a successful enterprise hasn't changed for hundreds of years', but there's no money in this fact for the gurus. They only make money from new models, paradigms, processes and techniques, no matter how bizarre, on the back of which they can peddle their books and speaking engagements.

To make my point, let's take one 'hot', current global theory to create high performance teams through bonding – 'Hugging in the workplace'. Charlie Footy and Bo Ajar, in their two separate books, 'Who Stole my Crackers?' and 'Paradigm Lost', both came to the same conclusion about what the ultimate management and leadership technique to build more effective teams is. The technique, fully validated by research into species in harsh environments, is hugging. It has sparked a worldwide academic leadership movement and a race to bring out the best learning media to ensure the ultimate workplace hug.

FREEDOM from BOSSES FOREVER

Encouragement of hugging at work has been shown to improve profitability, but what immediately irked owners of small businesses in the UK was the Government's eagerness to impose hugging regulations on all businesses with more than 5 employees, in order to improve UK productivity. Hence, within six months of the publication of Footy and Ajar's findings, legislation had been tabled making it a statutory condition for all employees (anyone employed for more than 16 hours a week – sole traders and partnerships not exempt) to receive entitlement to a 'hug a day from a co-worker of their choice'.

Furthermore, a government steering group was formed to oversee pilot and pathfinder projects to give all business owners £1000 each to help with the development of their 'hug friendly policies'.

Now, I know that one of TR's big Yorkshire friends, Sydney Bird, MD and owner of Britain's largest manufacturer of Pontefract cakes and all things liquorice, was one of the first small business 'experts' to be appointed to the government steering group to roll out the legislation and stimulate demand for hug-friendly policies.

Sydney is one of the world's great worriers; the kind who goes back to check locks and lights in his house at least four times before leaving, who tries on several outfits before choosing the same blazer and slacks he always wears and arrives at events at least two hours early so as not to be late. I rang Sydney from the train to ask him firstly, whether he agreed with the research findings?

"I've been ready and waiting for your call Leonora. Yes, there is a lot of research to show happy workers are more productive, but I'm one worker who isn't really very happy about hugging. Nor am I that happy about Government regulating and intervening in this area. Is it really a market failure if we're not hugging enough in the workplace?

I also have severe doubts about whether hugging legislation can be enforced. I know this might be a gender-specific thing, but I think it's a good idea to ask permission before you do multiple hugging. I'm a product of a Yorkshire family where the words 'can I give you a big hug?, (or worse, 'a big kiss?') were statements of terrifying intent from usually rather large, heavily powdered and perfumed aunts. The thought of such close, but unrefusable encounters inspires intense fright and flight reactions in me and in millions of other Northern menfolk.

My reservations about workplace hugging are not only influenced by my experiences with suffocating relatives. I am in the lowest ten percentile of the population for spatial awareness and physical co-ordination. A bit like my mate Tony Robbo, I notice that my awkwardness now goes before me and women in particular don't like me getting too close to them. When I enter a room women just smile weakly and wave at me from behind a table, pillar, plant or bystander.

I'm a great supporter of team building as an important part of business life, although again, when I regularly participate with Robbo in such activities as walking over hot coals (at your friend Ant Cracie's events), free fall parachute jumping, white water rafting and even go-kart racing, I'm usually asked to do it miles away from my colleagues. This is because I have a habit of causing injury to others in many unlikely ways, which rather defeats the 'bonding' aspect of the activity.

I admit that when participating in or watching sport, my team mates, friends and family can get a hug of delight from me after an exciting incident. However, I have my doubts that this shared spontaneity, with others you know well, is the same thing as the day-to-day hugging of work colleagues.

What is now being proposed by the occupational psychologists and to be legislated for by Government could create massive absenteeism in small businesses, as the thought of hugging the usual suspects day after day will lead to severe stress and depression in some. In fact, in the government's promotional film on the value of 'hugging circles', despite their company's business results supposedly having rocketed, most of the men filmed looked scared stiff to me.

FREEDOM from BOSSES FOREVER

Certainly hugging could prove a very dodgy activity, even if you've never had aunts like mine. It is a behaviour that will encourage your work colleagues who like the 'touchy feely' stuff for either 'warm fuzzy', sexual or barmy reasons. We all know the risks with the sexual lot and predators are not gender specific. However, I venture to suggest that there will be most grief from the barmy lot.

There is always a work colleague, someone at best eccentric, at worst about to spontaneously combust, who wants to 'release' or 'share' something with you. I prefer them to keep it to themselves, but if you give them any encouragement – like a hug – I can guarantee they'll be 'releasing' and 'sharing' all over you.

You'll find that colleagues, partners, friends, relatives and all manner of pets, vegetation and food groups have conspired to make their life unbearable. This leaves you, the 'hugger', as the only person the 'huggee' can trust. As such, your new role in life must be to soothe their troubled brow, calm their stormy waters and attend pilates and synchronised swimming classes with them every Tuesday and Thursday night.

Indeed, there will come a time in this relationship when you will find yourself looking after their four cats, two snakes and the parrot that likes to be spoken to in piratical, eighteenth century English whilst both parties wear eye patches. This is all so the 'huggee' can go away for a much needed break, yet still persecute you with a regular helping of bizarre postcards and text messages. It is unlikely in this fraught, depressed, exfoliated and depilated state that you'll even get placed at the synchronised swimming championship.

So, is all this potential angst worth it for the sake of a hug at work? No thanks. I'm just going to take my turn at making the coffee, buying biscuits and helping others get their work done. Admittedly it's a low key way of gaining team harmony, happiness and increased productivity, but it does neatly sidestep the parrot!"

Gosh, like his mate 'Robbo', he can bang on! But he does make exceedingly good Pontefract cakes and I needed you to see what a top entrepreneur adviser to Government sounds like on a new policy and programme intended to benefit business. Barking!

This is why, from this point onwards, I will ensure that you will only gain advice and tips on going it alone from small business owners who 'have the T shirt' but of whom no-one has ever heard.

I promised you some Leonorisms from this chapter and I always deliver.

12. All successful entrepreneurs whom I've met work bloody hard and are very focused. They've all had to make sacrifices to succeed.

Only those who have inherited wealth or previously worked in government jobs can be said to have 'got rich quick'. From talking to the entrepreneurs before they go native, these are five essential abilities which you must acquire:

13. Winning business through sales and marketing.

Whatever the product or service you are thinking of offering, you must continually practice selling it to prospective customers. You might need to change the product or service offer if you find it too difficult to sell. Selling and looking after customers are your most vital skills – no customers = no business. Don't let the experts lull you into believing things like 'planning is the most important skill'. It isn't; but 'winning and keeping customers' through your own eff

14. Dealing with regulations.

This means be generally aware of the regulations around your own enterprise, but don't fall into the trap of trying to comply with it all. Comply only when you have to (loads of free websites to help). Get this wrong and you'll find that you're legal but bust, because you had no time or money left to start and run your business.

15. Managing cash flow and obtaining finance.

Beg, steal or borrow. Despite what Government says, the self employed and real small business owners don't like borrowing from banks or angels. It's like having another boss and that's just what you wanted to get away from. We do borrow from family, from credit cards (we know we shouldn't, but we do) and we do make deals with other business owners, customers, suppliers and friends to get money in advance. Forget all that balance sheet/ 'Finance for non financial managers' stuff: you can always get a cheap bookkeeper. As the business owner, you have to understand and do pricing, get the right margin, minimise costs, maximise sales revenue and estimate/ manage your cashflow. You cannot outsource or delegate any of these money matters.

16. Making deals to make margins (profit).

You are now a win/win deal-making machine and should spend 50% of your time on this. You need to get very good at it. In order to make deals, you have to find people and opportunities through technology and through personal networking.

17. Beating the competition.

Forget the recession and the doom and gloom. Instead look at someone or some enterprise that is succeeding, right now, in a similar market (customers you want) to the one in which you want to trade. Break down what they're doing, put these in priority order for success ('must dos' rather than 'nice to dos') and beat them bit by bit.

Chapter Three

The Magic of Drinking Big

I only drink to make other people more interesting

George Jean Nathan
Quoted in News Summaries (08/04 1958)

I find that for softer, modern lips a pinkish beige tone gives you that bit of colour, which you need in winter. I also think that a lot of the clothes I see worn by British women business owners are fashionable, but they've ruined the look by what they're wearing underneath.

A common mistake is that the bra is too loose on the back and too small in the cup. Watch out for that double boob look which happens when your cup is too small. It is of course nothing like as bad as men, lounging on sun beds, who've failed to pack all their tackle in the netting of their designer swimming shorts.

18. When you think about it, much of looking good is about how well you tuck your bits in.

The good news is that the gorgeous, obsessive, upbeat, former fax saleswoman and Disneyland chipmunk, now entrepreneur, Sarah Blakely, who created and runs the Spanx label is now doing for boobs what she's done for bottoms. Check out the Bra-llelujah bra.

I promised I'd update you in this chapter on what I've worked out to date about the mystery of the missing UK government millions/billions, or why the politicians, senior civil servants and fat cats get very rich whilst everything they touch turns to dust.

FREEDOM from BOSSES FOREVER

Looking back at my notes from previous visits to the UK, I think I can see some nuggets of gold in what I thought previously were two unrelated 'cases'.

The first came from an ugly scene I witnessed at the International Convention Centre in Birmingham in 2004. Brent Spaniel, a guru presenter on Euro Linguistic Programming (ELP), was interrupted by a continual relay of bizarre mobile ring tones from films based on comic book heroes. He finally cracked after the Superman theme was immediately followed by Batman and left the stage, hurling insults at the audience.

It was a shame, because as a technique ELP is now believed to have far more currency than its predecessor, NLP. I did, however, manage to apprehend one of the mobile phone insurgents, whom I recognised from an earlier time when we had been on the same train.

After an enforced 8 minute separation from his Blackberry, he broke down and spilled the beans on who was behind these business guru 'assassinations'.

I was not surprised to hear that a disgruntled ex-employee of super-hunk, motivational guru and g-spot hunter (well I can let him try!) Anthony Cracie, was the brains behind these outrages. Mrs Big's (not her real name) employment had been terminated because of her inability to track down receipts for incidental purchases of milk or paper clips. This was compounded by her insane winter habit of turning on the heating in the office, rather than putting on one or more of the corporate, communal, AC branded fleeces, which were always available.

After the tip off I was soon able to interrogate Mrs Big, who was another quick beans spiller. This is what she said to my question, 'Why did all this trouble happen to the gurus at breakfast events mainly?'

"I needed to recruit my team of insurgents and they had to look the part to enable them to be camouflaged at the gurus' events. So, the night before each event I visited pubs in the City. I was looking for youngish professionals, execs. and traders who had gone into the pub. after work and were now in the middle of a heavy session.

There was always a mixed bag of bankers, brokers and economic analysts and sometimes a few from the financial and business press. They'd get steamed in the pub and then go off to spend the early hours at a lap dancing club. What I knew was that all of them would be willing to kill for a full English breakfast in the morning! I provided the full English and they did the 'killing' (at least the wrecking of the guru events). The rest is history".

Apparently, such was the severity of 'grunt' in her disgruntlement, that she vowed that Anthony Cracie and other star name business conference speakers would never again have an easy ride from an audience. Some, like TR, had been aware that he had recently been getting a fair amount of abuse from both his audience and the media, but hadn't really noticed much change from previously. Indeed, many thought that the distractions and interference when TR was speaking were making his presentations far more interesting than before.

Anyway, that's a summary of how I solved mystery one. The next mystery I solved was where £ millions of government money, earmarked to skill up and support prospective and existing small and home business owners, was going. It certainly wasn't getting to its destination.

Despite never having been a civil servant, TR usually stays at the Civil Service Club in Great Scotland Yard when overnight shelter in London is required. He likes it there, despite the small bore loos, screw topped wine and micro-waved chicken pies. He speaks very highly of all the staff. Anyway, he described enough of the place for me to become extremely suspicious about it. An evening visit proved particularly worthwhile for my investigation.

Every evening the club bar is occupied from early to closing time by the regulars. This motley crew drink more copiously as the evening progresses, their language deteriorates, the volume increases and riotous laughter is often punctuated by violent arguments. The multi talented and multinational bar team have to manage these mood swings each evening, whilst judging the merits of competing programme requests for the big screen TV. In addition to the regulars, the staff must attend to the sad, solitary, suited residents such as TR, and the elderly, retired civil servants who are in town for the Chelsea Flower Show, Wimbledon, Erotica at Olympia or other organised days out.

As the English say, 'suddenly the penny dropped'. I realised that the Civil Service Club is only posing as a Club – it is in fact a Care Home. It is a Care Home with an ulterior motive other than the welfare of the 'residents'. Its raison d'Être is to intern the 'residents' as often as possible in order to keep them away from the development or implementation of government policy. With the benefit of hindsight I should have come to this conclusion much faster. Sometimes I'm disappointed with my snail like deductive powers. Anyway, here is the rationale:

Q: Could these regulars earn enough to buy the amount of drink and food that they consume every night?

A: No way.

Q: Will these regulars be in a fit state to do their policymaking or policy implementing work the next morning?

A: No and even if they stagger across the road to their desks in Whitehall, they'll fall asleep rather than contribute to 'strategic decision making'.

Q: How many of the retired civil servants in the Club, enticed there by concessions on trips to races, shows, gardens, opera, dungeons and cricket, are actually Peers from the House of Lords whom the Government wants to discourage from speaking or voting?

A: Very many of them.

So how is this Guantanamo Bay for the grey suits whom Ministers want to sideline, funded? A small proportion – the odd few £million – is siphoned off every government programme from Education, to Defence, to Health. So I regard it is as pretty certain that between £10 million and £200 million of the money meant to assist entrepreneur training and development is, in fact, funding thousands of bottles of Johnnie Walker, assorted whips, rings, plugs and slings, together with extravagant gambling expeditions to horse races or orchid growing competitions.

That was how I solved mystery two. Now, to the untrained eye these two cases look unrelated, but that is because, back in the day when I solved these mysteries we didn't necessarily connect the following: *stopping those who are off message from talking or voting; highly paid speakers/consultants; stinking rich politicians; missing £billions; the City fat cats who don't care to look too closely at how their staff are making such big profits; annual bonuses that can buy mansions; and wealth creation policies that serve very few, getting through Parliament.* But we do now...

Poor Mrs Big: someone was pulling her strings and whoever it was must be well connected within the Civil Service. The Leonorism here is:

19. Effective networking is essential to the success of your enterprise. Choose productive online and offline networks from which you can learn, gain a profile and be given and give referrals.

Join a good business club, but be careful: choose the wrong one and you'll be wasting your valuable time with drunken peers or bouncy castle salesmen.

Oh! A very cute new replacement guard has joined us at Malton. Looks as if he works out, short blond hair and mischievous blue eyes. I could seek a liaison, but I haven't time. Shame: I could have got him to handcuff me to the bed for pretend ticket evasion. Every now and again getting back in touch with my submissive side is a

FREEDOM from BOSSES FOREVER

really good idea. What's not to like about men in uniform whose abs you can bounce coins off?

Now that's interesting too. In the Metro – that's the free paper which people leave on the racks, seats and floor, but never in the bin after they've read it – there is the following headline on page 5: 'Top Mandarins to Help Cameron'.

Basically it's about both a top welfare adviser to the Government and a Cross Bench Peer (whatever that means – either angry or painful?), once a Cabinet Secretary under Tony Blair, both going to help the Conservative party "to ensure that the shadow ministerial team and its policy programme would stand up to scrutiny if they won the next election". It is also reported that Ministers are struggling to attract fast stream civil servants (particularly the tall slim guys in the Boss suits – OK I made that bit up) because they do not want to be associated with an administration on its way out.

I've long suspected that the two party system in the US or UK is pretty irrelevant really, as the Ministers do what their key advisers and senior civil servants want them to do. It looks as though they've already started getting ready for the next lot.

Below this article (and Sydney Bird won't be altogether happy about this) is news that a UK technology firm (CuteCircuit) has developed a 'Hug Shirt' whereby the wearer presses sensors on their own body which connects with a mobile phone and transmits the 'hug' to the recipient. Then the really spooky bit! 'At a breakfast event last week, the new UK Trade and Investment Minister, Mervyn Davies, supporting CuteCircuit's hug shirts, told industry executives, "I would encourage you all to send hugs to politicians... as I have found out recently that when you become a politician you need lots of hugs." Heck, they're really taking this Hugging policy to the limits.

In the same paper was that, now famous, front row picture of all the celebs at a fashion show. Did you see me? I remember it well. It was Dolce & Gabbana's show in Milan. The press picture was of Elsa Pataley, Caterina Murino, Claudia Shiffer, Eva Herzigova, Nadja

Avermann (wearing what looked like one of Sir Jimmy Savile's tracksuits), Iluva Kendod, Lauren Hutton, Freida Pinto, Naomi Watts, Scarlett Johannson, Kate Hudson and Eva Mendes on the front row and I was just behind them, in the purple top. Anyway, they may all be beautiful but not always bright and beautiful. Iluva was sniffing a card from a mystery admirer and I heard her say 'Oooh… who do I know who smells of paper?'

At the show I met a senior English civil servant, who I'd better not name. He didn't look my idea of a senior English civil servant as he wore a black Armani suit, black faced watch with black leather strap, Paul Smith socks and tie but he did have the expected received pronunciation.

He said he was there on a buying mission for MPs' second homes and partners.

Naturally I asked 'What have you seen here that you like?'

He answered 'Claudia Shiffer'. They always do.

'For your buying mission?' I prompted.

'Oh' he said in a goldfish sort of way, 'the flooring, lighting, screens, mobile phones, PDAs, jewellery, cameras, cameramen, curtains, the building, shoes…that sort of thing…anything we can justify on allowances within the rules…definitely not clothes as there are rules against that as there are against exotic food, birds and sexual apparatus'.

I knew that what he was doing in 'topping up' MPs salaries with designer goodies, homes and perks is standard practice for you Brits. However, I was surprised that with the current public outrage, which makes Westminster look like a scene from the Crucible, that the practice could continue.

FREEDOM from BOSSES FOREVER

I couldn't resist asking him, 'Why not pay MPs a bigger salary, rather than spend so much money finding them extras which fit within these 'rules'?'.

"He said: 'Well, the problem is that a basic salary of £65k for an MP, £90k for a Junior Minister and £142k for a Minister really isn't much money at all, especially when they have to work a few days a week and quite a few weeks a year and in London too.'

I went: 'The problem?'

He went: 'Our problem is that there are many different factions in our society. There are a hell of a lot of people in the North who earn less than this and who are jealous. They think politicians get enough. My goodness, they'd be hopping mad if they realised that the £23k annual second home allowance, flipping and payment for personal advisers is really just the tip of the iceberg. The things that really make the difference are the pensions, expenses and all the freebies from big employers, institutions and other government bodies.' I went (you can see I've picked up my uber cool interviewing technique from Parky): 'And?'

He went: 'we call many of the freebies 'consultation' or 'employer-led' as the big employers tell us what policies and agencies they want and we make sure they get the support and funds from our policies and agencies so they can keep supporting them. It's a virtuous circle. Anyway, the real perks of the job are in the expenses, perks and huge pensions we receive. If the public only knew the half of it there'd be outrage.'

'What do you mean by factions?' I remember asking him, as it was a word with which I was unfamiliar.

'Oh, you know.... nurses, immigrants, people on benefits, those with disabilities, the over fifties, the workless... For instance, the UK has a big problem with one in seven of the adult workforce being self employed or running the own little business. Most of them have no choice but to do their own thing because they can't get proper jobs.

Anyway, they work over fifty hours a week on average for probably less than £20 grand a year. I know it's laughable, but all these minorities think that MPs and civil servants are already overpaid. In order to avoid their angst we have to do a bit of smoke and mirrors to ensure MPs get the things they need.'

'Can you still do that? I asked.

'Absolutely. It just needs different wiring. After this current outcry we'll have to come up with a new set of rules and procedures but we'll still find a way of allowing MPs and civil servants at least to double or even treble their income through expenses, allowances, pensions, second homes, trips and free meals. I'm just on an advance buying trip so we know what to get them after the new rules come in'

Of course I didn't know at this point what all this meant and why it was relevant to my assignment, but the two articles and the photo jogged my memory and rang my bell. Anyway, here we are at Scarborough station and here to help with my cases is Tony Robinson. I offer a fully outstretched hand for him to shake and stand well back from my cases:

20. Keep your distance from entrepreneurship gurus, particularly those with nil co-ordination.

Chapter Four

In Search of Essence of Scarborough

> *I tend to believe that cricket is the greatest thing that God ever created on Earth.... certainly greater than sex, although sex isn't too bad either*
>
> **Harold Pinter**
> Quoted in 'Quotable Quotes for Quoters by Aubrey Malone 2005

Despite its reputation for enterprise and cultural leadership, Scarborough can be relied upon as a very late adopter of fashion trends. They may not even be aware that leggings (as you Brits call them) are back this season, nor indeed that grey is the new black. In fact, I can get away with my Top Shop jeans as long as I wear my latest short mac. by Jasper Conran – grey/white naturally – my gold leather pumps by Jimmy Choo and my new, lime green leather bag from Mulberry.

What I'm wearing is still 'stand out' dressing in Scarborough and from the moment I step off the Stripping for Freedom train people will mutter to each other: "isn't she off the telly?" My only celebrity competition was the, now late, disgraced, Jimmy Savile who wore dodgy tracksuits.

An obvious Leonorism here for when you start your own enterprise:

21. Leave your old work clothes and corporate style behind you. You are now your brand so dress to impress.

I recommend that if you ever visit Scarborough you prepare a small survival kit. Firstly, you'll need to survive the screaming, giant seagulls – thousands of them – and you don't mess with a Scarborough seagull. Call me old fashioned, but I've always thought that piercing and tattoos make anybody look hard, but on a seagull they're positively menacing.

If one comes up to you and asks for a chip, my advice is to give them the bagful and run for it. It's fortunate that big, slouchy handbags look good, because when walking around Scarborough you should carry in them a pack of cigarettes and a can of lager to give you something to pay off any threatening seagull. (OK, so I made the cigarettes and lager bit up.)

Since I was last in Scarborough, the UK Government has awarded Scarborough the title of 'The Most Enterprising Place in Yorkshire' and then 'The Most Enterprising Place in Britain'. Scarborough received its award at 11 Downing Street and then at a ceremony in Prague was crowned most enterprising town in Europe. Quite remarkable for a town with a population of only 50,000 to beat off competition from major places such as Helsinki, Valencia and Liege. TR felt that if we tried to capture the essence of what makes Scarborough so enterprising, then we'd get lots of Leonorisms to pass on to you Strippers for Freedom.

Before that, I have a few minutes respite from the bearded one and just enough time to check my e-mails at my hotel. Joy of joys, there is a lengthy e-mail from Ant Cracie. As it is pertinent, I've reproduced it in full below:

'Babe, Hope you survived the train and then the TR greeting. Look, I've arranged for a nice guy called Stephen to meet you on behalf of the Tochen network at your hotel around 8 am for breakfast in the morning. You should be able to do a deal to speak at one of their big events. In advance, here are a few quick notes to help you:

The founder is HR Tochen (HRT). Family v. well connected – media, oil, construction, engineering, arms – sort of 'king makers' of most influential jobs in world. Family & close friends -Yale, Harvard, Oxford, Cambridge – influential circles like Bush dynasty, based on who you know, where you went to uni. all that kind of thing. You can be an imbecile (Hunter Thompson's word, not mine), but enrolled at birth into the right uni. and will find yourself in a powerful network

FREEDOM from BOSSES FOREVER

etc. HRT *launched/wrote papers/ spoke on christocracy concept: Christianity = democracy interchangeable, values, networks to diminish threats to christocracy etc. Bilderberg, Yale's Skull and Bones, Illuminati, Knights Templar perhaps, other networks certainly involved: a network of networks, online and offline. Hell, who knows? I don't, as there are always lots of rumours. Anyway, major leaders and wealthiest global folk getting together discussing world threats and opportunities kinda thing.*

In early eighties, HRT and some powerful friends started to join up all his thinking and networks. He saw multi billion/massive and v. quick growth of multilevel or referral networking worldwide (e.g. in UK in '84 one company alone had 2 × 10,000 crowds of agents in one day at NEC in Birmingham and was filling every major stadium in US.) HRT saw potential for global wealth creation club. Development type know how/ education/ prof. devpt. seems to be at the core. It's big on seminars and book (DVDs/CDs) club but no building, no executive, no website, no catalogues – all by invitation and word of mouth. Networking is prob. faster than ever because of social/business networking sites and other mobile comms. Oh and they also do some predominately male accessories too (you won't like these accessories babe).

There are different branches for different interest groups, including women, but I've only ever spoken to their Entrepreneurs' Club. It's very big and has worldwide influence. People make money, but never sure whether it's the Tochen network. They're not really a secret, but world's press say v. little and they don't have spokespeople, buildings or publications, so guess they'll never be news.

The very top leaders (top of every downline – they talk uplines and downlines – it's nothing to do with coke) are not likely to go to public meetings, (security) but we can guess by some of the speakers they attract that there are some pretty powerful dudes involved. Oh, and a curious thing, not sure if it's a rumour, but heard that UK rather than US is where they first launch new stuff. Something about two-thirds of all CCTV cameras manufactured end up in UK.

So what do they like about your 'Bong in the Orange Grove'? Well, seems like they really go for that left hand side of the brain shaking the right hand side, through shaking hands with yourself, the smiling rapidity bit and the emo-toe/working feelings/from ground upwards stuff. You see they're really big on personal development leading to business or organisational development and these are the kind of speakers and books they promote.

Hope that helps. Give Stephen a hello from me (but if it's a kiss then only a little one).

Ciao, Ant

OK, that can wait until tomorrow morning. Let's get back to the most Enterprising place in Britain – Scarborough.

Well I can certainly see why Scarborough is the most enterprising place award winner. All the new street furniture, creation of a café society, new marina, developments of smart holiday homes, real homes and leisure facilities in the North and South Bays. There's even a new Creative and Cultural Centre for creative entrepreneurs, writers, designers, artists, web people etc. to work in and all very modern and hi tech. I love the free Wi-Fi provided for everyone at the seafront too. It means you can have a coffee on the beach or on a boat and still do your work on your laptop/netbook/smartphone/Android/iPad – OMG whatever. Cool.

What's really interesting to me though, is that they've kept all the traditional entertainments too and they still 'pack 'em out'. It would be very wise of you to visit Scarborough to learn a bit from all the successful business owners in the town.

There are a number of famous Yorkshire business people that have built successful independent careers from very inauspicious starts to life and tough backgrounds. The traits they have are worth adopting for all strippers for freedom.

22. They are enterprising (go into situations others would regard as risky).

23. They are brilliant self-promoters (see chapter 8 for more tips).

24. They have passion and integrity which makes them frank and forthright with an unshakeable sense of what is right.

25. They are highly 'professional' (meet every commitment), exceptionally hard working and self sufficient.

26. They totally believe they can make their own luck.

Much of the traditional Scarborough entertainment for the tourists has changed very little in the last 100 years and yet it's still bringing in the punters. I'm amazed really, but if you sample it to learn from it, then my survival guide to this traditional entertainment will come in handy.

Make no mistake, there is some top entertainment. There are first class, original plays performed in the round at the Stephen Joseph Theatre and top music and comedy stars, ballet and opera appearing at the Futurist Theatre. The Spa complex hosts many great concerts and one of the UK's finest Jazz Festivals. There's Europe's largest Open Air Theatre which brings top pop acts and there are many festivals of all styles of music, drama, food and drink including a literary festival, sea festival and coastal festival bringing all the arts together.

However, it's the entertainment that is unique to Scarborough to which I want to give you a guide. You are warned, however, that patrons of this traditional entertainment have been known to develop serious medical conditions.

The top four of the many 100 year or older attractions of which to be wary are; summer season variety shows, county cricket at North Marine Road, football matches at the McCain Stadium (now defunct) and naval battles at Peasholm Park. All these venues have bars in the vicinity and many people who haven't been warned what to expect at these events are tempted to drink themselves into oblivion. This is not advisable, as the memories will always return and returning memories mean that alcoholism will be the inevitable result.

Avoiding the attraction is the best advice I can give you. I also understand that you can't always prevent yourself being dragged by a local into attending and so it is essential that I give you the preferred antidote or treatment for each of the top four. Put these lifesavers in your survival pack to carry with you when you are out and about in Scarborough:

Summer Season Variety Shows take place mainly in the evening at the Spa or Futurist theatres. They are not to be confused with shows with a headline act or acts of which you've heard and have therefore chosen to see because of their stars.

Instead, the summer season variety shows will be sold to you by entrepreneurs, through sizzling titles and descriptions which mask the lack of substance. You'll see words like 'back by popular demand', 'spectacular', 'back to the good old days', 'hugely entertaining', 'award winning' and 'undoubtedly Scarborough's number one...'. You'll also be promised clean comedians, dazzling dancers, songs to sing along with, surprising sets and colourful costumes.

There will always be a speciality act of either a ventriloquist with a lisp, a magician with a clumsy assistant, a half hearted juggler with a faulty music tape and an animal act that just doesn't care anymore.

Usually the entertainer/promoter of the show will star in a 'tribute to the musicals' segment. With said entertainer/promoter being in their sixties or seventies, the advisability of them being Mary Poppins doling out a 'Spoonful of Sugar' to the young dancers, dressed as children, is always questionable.

The point is, this will never be entertainment as you recognise it and you can easily start to worry about 'the meaning of life', 'running out of time' and care homes. Certainly, it will be a highly stressful two

FREEDOM from BOSSES FOREVER

hours. I suggest that you don't come back into the auditorium after the interval.

Just tell your companions afterwards, that on checking your mobile during the break, you found out that you had an urgent domestic cat crisis to deal with. So, to get through the first half of the show unscathed, what do you need in your survival kit? The answer is magic mushrooms – simple really.

County Cricket at North Marine Road; As a Canadian, I understand little about cricket. The most difficult thing to understand is that after playing a game for nearly a week, there can be no winner or loser and the crowd doesn't care. Apparently the greatest writer and commentator on cricket, John Arlott, rarely described the play, mainly the players and the view, and was an even better writer on wine, which he sampled all day so that he was capable of falling asleep well before the day's end. I now know that Yorkshire is the biggest county in England and the common passion of its people is for cricket. It is more than just a sport to the 'Tykes' as they're called.

Some of it is frankly as unintelligible as the 'flat 'atted chap' shouting out to sell his newspapers, scorecards and goodness knows what. Everything I've learned has been through my conversations with genial hosts Trevor, Jean and Andrea but I've forgotten much as, like Arlott found, there is a soporific effect of the wine at the end of a long day. It makes the next day's education all the more fun though as it all seems brand new.

Anyway, I'll have a go at explaining. There are only two venues in Yorkshire to watch the county cricket club perform. Both have hosted Yorkshire cricket since the 1890s. One is usually empty, ugly, wet, overpriced, feeds beer drinking carnivores only, employs stewards to ruin your day and is in Leeds. The other is full, beautiful, sunny, multicultural, happy, welcoming, plentiful in varied food/drink and is in Scarborough.

Scarborough cricket ground is as good as its cinder toffee ice cream (mmmmm what's not to like about cinder toffee ice cream in a chocolate dipped cone?). So what can be the danger to your health? The answer is that those seeking peer recognition or those of an impressionable nature can suffer a complete personality change. They enter the ground at 10.30 a.m. as an individually fashionable, carefree, positive member of one sex and leave at 6.30 p.m. as a cloned, obsessive, miserable member of the opposite sex.

Those who conform easily will be affected less and will leave the ground fairly anonymously, wearing garish, baggy replica team shirts that they've bought at lunchtime from the club shop. However, some women will be converted to wearing sunburned noses, floppy hats, stripy ties, ill fitting blazers and soup stained, light chinos while some men will be moved to wearing make up, pink or white baseball hats, large sunglasses, pastel coloured short sleeved tops, floral skirts and open toed sandals.

How does this conversion happen? First, you must recognise that a high proportion of Yorkshire people come to Scarborough cricket ground to talk continuously and not watch any cricket at all. The 'non watchers' are there either to talk about cricket in the past, eat bacon butties, organise bets and drink beer, or to talk about their friends and work colleagues in the present, organise a picnic, drink wine and knit woolly jumpers. There are many unfathomable traditions; like everyone missing the last 90 minutes' play as the B&Bs at which they're staying refuse to provide the evening meal after 5.30 p.m.

Some find their historical cricketing knowledge is not up to membership of the former group and others find their knitting competence prevents them being in the latter. Hence the desire to change personality, dress and peer group by the end of the day.

So, if you want to be in the former 'talking cricket' group, and wish to remain in your original state and seat throughout the day, you'll need to put into your survival pack a copy of '100 Yorkshire County Cricket Club Greats' (price £12.00). Be sure to bookmark, for ease of reference, the entries for Hawke, Hirst, Rhodes, Hutton, Yardley, Trueman, Gough, Lehmann, Root, Bairstow, Sidebottom (what

FREEDOM from BOSSES FOREVER

strange names!) and Lyth. Alternatively, if you want to be in the 'not cricket' talking group, then be sure to pack some heavily sherried trifles and, if you can't improve your knitting in time, just bring a selection of patterns on which to ask your companions' opinion.

Scarborough Football Club now plays in Bridlington, but is hoping to return to Scarborough soon. I'll tell you my experience, so you can be prepared for its return to either the original or the new stadium. This isn't 'the beautiful game' as you may have seen it played on television. Nevertheless they do have a proven formation, which allows them consistently to lose or draw and score a maximum of one goal at each home game.

They're nicknamed the Seadogs and used to play at the Theatre of Chips (McCain Stadium). They play in such tough leagues that even the watching seagulls have been known to flinch as the tackles fly in.

You will not be able to understand the particular insults that the Scarborough fans hurl at officials and opposition players. However, you can be sure that each insult will include the 'f' word, eyesight or a bodily orifice and 'donkeys on the beach'.

The mince and pea pie with chips is revered as the top dish to eat whilst standing and watching the match. Only locals know its unique recipe, as only they live long enough to pass it on to the next generation. However, watching Scarborough play can become addictive and this leads to high blood pressure and clinical depression.

To prevent falling foul of these conditions, it is important to put in your survival pack your MP3 player. Then, on entering the ground, buy a programme and plug in to your MP3. Amuse yourself by spending the whole match trying to translate the programme into English. Do not switch off the music, take your earpieces out or let your eyes wander from the printed page until the ground is completely empty of people and seagulls. Then you may leave.

Tony Robinson OBE (with Soculitherz)

The Naval Battle at Peasholm Park; for at least eighty years, twice weekly, there is a full, entrance fee paying congregation to see the naval combat of miniature warships, on Peasholm Park lake. When I say miniature, some of the warships have to be large enough to carry a live, six foot person inside them, as is revealed, to gasps of amazement, at the end of the show. (TR still gasps in amazement and he's seen it over 30 times already).

Some have questioned the educational and cultural value of integrating the naval conflicts and opposing nations of both world wars and the Falklands into one big, noisy battle. However, the US air force could learn about precision bombing from the coat-hanger planes that zoom down on wires.

There are explosions, fires and fireworks from the bombardment of battlements, warships and supply vessels. It is a thoroughly absorbing spectacle. However, it is not this action but the presenter of the show who should carry the health warning. It is one of the great mysteries of the 20th and 21st centuries that the same presenter has survived, played with his organ and introduced this show to over ten successive generations of holidaymakers.

His 'warm up' organ medleys of popular wartime tunes can induce both hysteria and incontinence in his audience. This is not as dangerous as the physical and mental deterioration that can occur when he speaks to the audience. You need to know that he will speak before the show, during the show, as he commentates on the conflict and warships, and after the show.

His patter can be lethal for those suffering heart or stress related conditions. You can become disorientated very quickly, as you will not know whether what he's saying is a threat, a joke or a plea for help. All his remarks will be greeted by total silence, even though the audience can feel increasingly guilty about not laughing. He builds this mass, mutual, guilt complex by finishing each tale with either: "that one always makes me chuckle", or "that was a private joke between me and myself".

The 'boys and girls' in the audience whom he is encouraging to participate in booing and cheering various parts of the action, will also become confused and increasingly violent. Parents initially attempt to motivate good behaviour by buying ice creams for their offspring. Unfortunately his patter seems never-ending, so that parents and grandparents finish by joining their little ones in throwing any objects that come to hand, including walking sticks, at the presenter.

Elderly visitors, (now without their walking sticks), and their escorts are most at risk. Insidiously, through his music, community singing and commentary he rekindles their wartime memories. Then, the sights and sounds turn the memories into a tangible, new reality. Inevitably, therefore, at the point in the show where the planes zoom down from behind the audience, chaos and carnage will ensue. Some will fall as they flee to the air raid shelters, others will be mown down by the scooters and wheelchairs and some just end it all by jumping in the lake.

Against this backdrop of flailing limbs, screams, groans, explosions, fires and organ music you may feel yourself descending into hell, or bedlam, or both. Fortunately, you will have packed my top cure in your survival pack. It is a loaded gun with a silver bullet. Shoot the presenter in the heart and normality will return. He'll be back for the next show, but at least you'll have survived and you will certainly never repeat your naval battle experience.

There's a saying in these parts which is: 'There's nowt so funny as folk'. Your customers may often have difficulty in explaining what they want, what they like and what they're prepared to pay for:

27. To be a successful entrepreneur, running your own show, you don't always need to be particularly innovative but you do need to know what will attract paying customers. Like the Scarborough entertainment: 'if it works, keep doing it'.

28. Look for customer offers that work and copy them, adding your unique little twist (a brand, a price, a colour, a guarantee, a new location, a new way of distribution, packaging etc).

So cut out and keep this little survival guide for when you visit, and learn from the most Enterprising Place in Britain. It is a real treat and so good is it that I suggested to the protagonists responsible for the renaissance that they should adopt the Vegas slogan i.e. *'What happens in Scarborough, stays in Scarborough'*.

Next up, in the interests of research for all you strippers for freedom, I'd arranged to go to a show with Tommy Tatlow that evening. Tommy is a Scarborough entrepreneur, boating lake owner, part time DJ, announcer at major events like strongman, sea shanty, jumping off the pier in fancy dress, cross dressing raft races etc (not simultaneously) and a replacement commentator for the naval battle at Peasholm Park, should the regular one succumb to a major injury from walking sticks and tupperware boxes hurled by the audience.

Although Tommy is a revered character now in Scarborough, he's originally from Grimethorpe. He wasn't quite as revered in Grimethorpe for, as the second euphonium player in their band, he objected to them recruiting a Lancastrian as principal conductor, especially with a first name of Elgar. Anyway, eventually he had to leave after being caught in an illicit liaison with one of the colliery boss's wives. Unforgivable, especially during the miners' strike. He was found out a bit like Monica Lewinsky's blue cocktail dress and the DNA in the sticky stuff: they found some of Tommy's false teeth in her pinny, (pinny = pinafore/sort of apron). It was a perfect match with the gaps in his top set.

To come back from this scandal, (OK not quite as big a come-back as Bill Clinton retaining the Presidency plus £60 million in speaking fees), is some achievement and this is why Tommy's advice is worth 'summat'. Leonorism:

29. Never have an affair with your best customer's spouse.

FREEDOM from BOSSES FOREVER

Tommy and I went to the Futurist theatre in Scarborough to see a marvellous ballet of the Nutcracker Suite with Grigorovich's choreography. We got there a little late, as I had to ask Tommy T to change what he was wearing. Indeed, it took five changes before he found something that I could tolerate being seen with and I never did get him to take off his braces and 'flat 'at'. Despite this shaky start it turned into a magnificent evening, with a full orchestra and over 60 in the corps de ballet of the Moldavian National Ballet.

Although I've been to Sir Alan Ayckbourn's wonderful Stephen Joseph Theatre many times to see theatre in the round (do also see the sublime Northern Broadsides), this was only the second time I'd been in the Futurist theatre, which holds over two thousand. Despite its slightly run down appearance, it has a large stage with superb lighting and sound, and with a full house and our great view from the circle of this wonderful and colourful spectacle, it became a magical place.

I suppose I must admit to just a little tinge of something not always 'comme il faut', when watching beautiful ballerinas being swept off their feet by muscled and lithe Adonii. I think that this 'something' is envy about how impossibly slim, fit and serene they are. I bet that even if they had six large bags of Maltesers before the show they'd burn off all the calories by the end of it.

But they were wonderful and as we were having a drink after the show I suggested to Tommy that there can't be many times a year that such top quality entertainment leads to a packed Futurist. Tommy took his pipe out of his mouth, (he can't smoke it, but it's ready loaded for when we get outside), and explained that the next weekend would be a sell-out for an equally high quality performance when the Chuckle Brothers (Barry and Paul, apparently) performed 'Dr What and the Return of the Garlics' followed by 'Chuckle Trek, the Lost Generation'. I don't know them, although I had heard reference in the media that they were as unlikely a pairing as the protestant, Rev Ian Paisley and catholic, Martin McGuinness power sharing in Northern Ireland.

What was important was that Tommy gave me some tips about pricing to make a profit. His example was in the entertainment industry, but I think the tips are applicable to all sectors.

He explained that the ballet company would receive 2000 x an average £20 a head. From this £40,000 they would have to pay the theatre, their marketing and travel costs and the wages of a company of 120. The following week, the Chuckle Brothers would receive 2000 x an average £10 a head, but they would probably make far more profit, as their £20,000 would cover similar theatre costs, but fewer marketing costs – probably no more than 10 people's wages and less in transportation costs. They would also sell a huge amount of merchandise when they signed autographs after the show.

Tommy asked me to assume that both companies could put on the same number of shows each year and that most of these shows would be at much smaller venues. It looks as if both have successful and profitable business models, with a great offer, but within their offer *charging the right price* is absolutely crucial to their success.

Tommy said that:

30. It is essential to set the right price for your product or service when you first start out in your own business. It can adversely affect your business if you get the price wrong and have to change it, as this will shake potential customer confidence in the true value of your product or service.

So, he says *charging the right price involves more than just researching what others charge for something similar*. It requires ensuring that your price covers the cost to produce the work or service, plus the cost of gaining the customer and getting the product/ service to the customer, plus *the maximum profit margin you can achieve*. Tommy reckons that most first time business owners/ entrepreneurs, in their desperation for initial customers, charge too low a price at the beginning.

31. It's about getting innovative about your pricing, by seeing where there is a market gap in providing your service or product in a way that will both be highly valued by the customer and may often avoid direct price comparisons with your competitors.

32. If you're in doubt, then aim high. You can always discount for volume or by negotiation with the customer, but you must leave leeway in your pricing to cover future business eventualities, such as taking on staff, contractors, premises or equipment and even for lean periods.

So being *price perfect is essential*. Build the price up through unique customer value and differentiation and the above tips should ensure you don't make the very common mistake of people going it alone for the first time by being 'me-too' or under pricing.

Dear fellow strippers, I think you'll agree that Tommy's tips on pricing are useful. As he was speaking I was certainly moving my fee rate upwards for the unique service I offer. What I also spared you were Tommy's remarks, quoted verbatim. Instead, I translated and interpreted for you. I'm sure that Tommy and TR are the kind of 'banging on all the time' folk who will have been locked away in the Peasholm Park Boathouse when the judges for the most enterprising places in Britain, and Europe, visited Scarborough. Maybe they should have thrown away the key.

Tony Robinson OBE (with Soculitherz)

Chapter Five

The Naked Reader

I think nudity in films is disgusting. But if I were 22 with a great body, it would be artistic, tasteful and a progressive religious experience

Shelley Winters
Quoted in 'Quotable Quotes for Quoters by Aubrey Malone 2005

If you're one of the many thousands of my readers who have bought an expensive pair of opaque tights that have now gone bobbly around the heels, never fear: there are at least three ways to continue maximising your investment. Firstly, use a sharp pair of scissors to cut the feet off and use them as leggings. Secondly, wear your tights with boots or thirdly, cut the legs into round strips and use them as hairbands. Bugger, why didn't I think of Spanx?!

As per Ant's instructions, I met Stephen at the Royal Hotel for breakfast. He was staying here and he wasn't difficult to recognise. He was by far the best looking guy in the hotel. Late twenties to early thirties, tall, slim, fair hair and wearing a very smart, light grey suit with a light blue shirt, cufflinks, but no tie. Only downside was he was wearing one of those 'executive' hundred dollar watches you see advertised in the Sunday supplements.

Anyway, quite a dishy package with whom to spend the early morning in a rather old fashioned but very pleasant, spacious dining room with silver service. He got right to the point.

'Leonora, thanks for coming.'

'Mon plaisir. What label is your suit?'

FREEDOM from BOSSES FOREVER

'Boss: why do you ask?'

'It's the business I'm in. I like checking out my hunches.'

'Hey, fine. Look Leonora, I'll cut right to it. I've been asked by some friends in the Tochen network if you and Ant would be willing to speak at one of our events in the next few weeks. We love your work. In fact, 'Bong in the Orange Grove' is now one of our recommended books'.

'Have you read it?'

'Certainly. Hey look, you've upset me. I'm mortally wounded that you can't tell I've been practising your rapid smiling exercises in mirrors, shop windows, shiny shoes – any chance I get.'

'Ha... flatterer. Have you a fee in mind?'

'Of course. You'd receive a single, up front payment of twenty two thousand US dollars each, which also covers your expenses for booking your own flights and hotel for one or two nights. So how much you spend is up to you and the venue is in Madrid, so lots of flights there. You'll have to be available to speak to about six hundred members and their guests on the evening. About an hour and a half show, between the two of you. Then the next morning you'll attend a breakfast meeting with about twenty of the leading members and their guests.

'So that's two different presentations on consecutive days?'

'No, you don't need to prepare anything for the breakfast, as it'll be a facilitated discussion and you'll just be asked questions by the attendees. The breakfast session will last between forty five and seventy five minutes. How does it all sound so far?'

'OK I think. What's Ant said?'

'He's cool about it. He's already spoken at a Tochen UK event and loved it. It's a very positive audience – nice people.'

''Usually I name the terms.'

'I know, but what I'm authorised to offer you is a bit above what you'd normally charge for this kind of show, especially as it'll lead to more sales of your book too. Most speakers feel that accepting an opportunity to attend or speak at a Tochen network event is a 'Yes, please', no brainer type of decision.

'But I've never heard of Tochen.'

'Cool. Sorry about that. Didn't Ant tell you anything? What do you want to know?'

'Who'll be in the audience?'

'Sure. Well look, there are four branches of the Tochen network and the majority of the meetings are on a branch by branch basis. The Madrid meeting is for the Entrepreneurs' club branch. So, members and their guests will all be successful business owners or leaders of enterprise and commerce – nice people – your kind of people'.

'It's not network or multi level marketing/pyramid selling is it? I hate all that happy clappy, achieve your dreams, get rich rubbish. Anyway, it's illegal in Canada and I am a Canadian citizen.'

'No it's not that at all. I can't deny it's a network, but no one gets commissions for selling anything. Neither can you apply to join it, as you have to be invited. Members only pay their annual subscriptions to a charity of their choice if they feel they're getting value for it and anyone can leave the network at any time.'

'Not a religious sect is it?'

'No, although one of the four key values includes being 'Christian'. That only means the network goes by the values prescribed in the

FREEDOM from BOSSES FOREVER

Bible – quicker than writing some out. In fact, nothing is written – no rules, regulations, agreements or paperwork. It's all about development and person-to-person. We just enjoy our network and enjoy developing. No prayer meetings and no-one has to go to church – I promise!'

'How long have you been in it?'

'No-one says whether they're in it or not. I've just been asked to see if you'd like to speak with Ant at the Madrid event. Look, I have to dash Leonora. Why not have a chat with Ant, see if you want to do it and he'll get hold of me to let me know? Naturally breakfast is paid for and don't feel you have to rush. Great meeting you and I hope that the next time we meet it'll be in Madrid.'

Good looking guy, but a bit intense I thought.

Here's an extract from *'Buzzing with the Entrepreneurs'*. There are two reasons why I give you this extract, dear reader. The first is because I'm absolutely furious with Ant for getting me mixed up with this Tochen network stuff. I really do hate it.

It does sound just like that network marketing where gullible people spend thousands on non refundable training from their 'uplines', who have persuaded them they could get rich by recruiting others whom they influence to buy stock 'in advance'. They see themselves making more money if they buy the stock to gain a higher position in the network. People fill their garages with stock and then lose their houses when everyone finds their investments aren't paying off, nothing is moving and no real money is earned in the network.

This is just like what's happened with the banks. Senior executives have no idea what's really going on; they just allow people to gamble on everyone else keeping buying and what they've bought being of value. The bosses take the credit and the minions take the risks and rewards until some of the numbers don't come up.

Tony Robinson OBE (with Soculitherz)

The second reason is that this extract will remind us all of the time I first realised that Ant Cracie was hot and whilst I'm trying to regain my cool after meeting Stephen, I hope that it will make me think better of him. Think of this as a flashback for when they make the movie of this book. As the Abba soundtrack has been used up, then I hope they use the Stones for my film. If they do, then this flashback will be accompanied by 'Let's Spend the Night Together'. Corny I know, but so is the sublime Mama Mia. There are also a number of good tips for you Strippers for Freedom. Enjoy.

"These rail companies know everything there is to know about piling on the agony. If you can get a seat, you settle down in the hope of avoiding the journey from hell. Within seconds you know that hope was a forlorn one. The first announcement lets you know that staff shortages mean no trolley service. The second informs you that a failure to pick up supplies means little choice of food or drink, even if you beat the odds by fighting your way to be served at the buffet car before your stop.

Regular announcements will follow to let you know that high winds, signal failures, speed restrictions, platform congestion, awaiting replacement crew, sick drivers, sick passengers, sick jokes or any combination of these are conspiring to make your estimated arrival time later and later.

Each carriage will also be given a handful of tone deaf but self taught, 'musical' drunks and at least four of the most miserable kids in Britain, all record holders in sustained wailing. You will always be seated next to 'Mr Mobile Phone User of the Year' who has flu, the plague, rotting feet and spends every non coughing and sneezing minute patronising his staff, clients and family with tales of his machismo lifestyle. There surely must have been an opportunistic colleague who could have found some scissors when he went bungee jumping?

I must admit that, if I noticed anyone in first class whom I could usefully interview for this book, I immediately upgraded. Once, I truly struck gold. As I was hiking up the platform at Kings Cross to

FREEDOM from BOSSES FOREVER

get to coach B for (jokingly) 'B Quiet', I noticed the celebrity business guru, Anthony Cracie, in first class.

I'd met Cracie earlier in the year at an awards event where he scooped the 'Business Guru of the Year Award'. Cracie is famous for his weekend seminars, which always include getting senior managers to do 'Fire Walking', or a variation he's currently piloting. Instead of walking over hot coals, it's called the 'Cut Toenails Walk'. Something to do with overcoming, prejudice and decorum, as well as fear.

Most executives think they'll never have the guts to do 'The Walk', but by the end of the weekend, all eight hundred or so delegates, paying £2000 each for the privilege, cut their toenails and deposit them in a one by ten inches trough, – about the length of a cricket pitch. Then, one by one, with the tension and camaraderie increasing, they proceed to walk over the toenails. A remarkable feat of mind over, well, feet matter!

Cracie is American, but you Brits often mistakenly assume that Canadians and Americans share similar values and therefore have a special relationship, like the Brits with Yanks. No way! You must remember that although I am now pretty much a global celebrity (and certainly an international fashion icon), I am first and foremost a proud Canadian. I've used the following short transcript from a radio conversation between Canadians and Americans off the coast of Newfoundland to explain the difference and I'm sure you, dear readers, will enjoy it too:

Americans: 'Please divert your course 15 degrees north to avoid collision'

Canadians: 'Recommend you divert your course 15 degrees south to avoid collision'

Americans: 'This is the Captain of a US Navy ship. I say again, divert your course.'

Canadians: 'No. I say again, you divert your course.'

Americans: 'This is the aircraft carrier USS Lincoln, the second largest ship in the United states Atlantic fleet. We are accompanied by three destroyers and three cruisers. I demand you change your course 15 degrees north, or counter measures will be undertaken to ensure the safety of this ship.'

Canadians: 'This is a lighthouse. Your call.'

Anyway, despite being American, Cracie is also a bit of a hunk and I had no hesitation in going to sit next to him. Joie de joie! When I got there, he was also sitting next to Wal Whiteside, a celebrity business speaker in his own right, who was a previous winner of the BAB 'Inspirational Business Innovator of the Year Award'

The atmosphere in the first class carriage of the 6.30 train from London to Edinburgh is buzzing with charisma. I am seated across the table from two of the most 'in demand' speakers at premier business events.

I'd last seen them both in action at the Scarborough Spa Complex. Whiteside, from Carntplae in Lancashire, with the transatlantic accent, is noted for leaving his audiences numb at the end of his presentations. His publicity says 'he dazzles, distracts and always delivers'. Perhaps more attractively, Cracie, from Little Rock, Wyoming, simply ignites his audiences as he gets them to 'visionate'. Visionating is similar to urinating, but, as Cracie so aptly puts it, "I teach you to see further than you can pee".

Both Whiteside and Cracie have forthright styles that could, but don't, offend and I asked them first up "What does it take to be an all time great presenter?" Wal Whiteside answered: "Good question Leonora. I put it down to something in my genes, but I also have a device for building the tension. Firstly, I like to whisk my audience into a kind of emotional bubble bath, by giving them my life story of how a wretched childhood, a lost conker and a psychopathic boss drove me to entrepreneurship, innovation and fulfilment.

FREEDOM from BOSSES FOREVER

Then, I get them to laugh with me at my early failures and finally I get them to realise and weep at how they could, but just failed to have my billion dollar idea to make toilet roll holders into interactive communication centres. I sometimes use that Spanx woman example too – cutting the feet off your tights."

Anthony Cracie chipped in here, "I agree with Wal; it is a great question Leonora. My approach is different from Wal's, as I get my message across through outstanding models. By this, I don't mean the 'Cracie Babes' who carry my props onto the stage, but the memorable new concepts to which I introduce my followers and which they must put into action. An example of this would be my coat hanger theory of how best to select vision-ates.

Vision-ates are managers whom you can be sure will increase profits through increasing sales and reducing costs. This is one of my favourite ways of improving business performance. I liken the new recruit to a smart, casual jacket. The left sleeve is sales and the right sleeve is costs. If you put a coat hanger in the jacket, you can get a smooth, straight effect at the top. These are exactly the qualities you want from your new recruit.

On the other hand, if you take the coat hanger out, then the sleeves and the jacket crumple and lose shape. This you don't want. So this means that when you're recruiting, what you want to look out for are balanced candidates, both straight and smooth, who are able to see sales and costs as two arms, but under different shoulders. I admit it is a simple concept, but it has to be for them to remember it the next day, back in their little cubicles with their cappuccino lifestyles. They just love it and me".

I must admit to being mesmerised by just how articulate they were (especially Cracie). It sounded more like soul music than the spoken word, but I recovered in order to ask my next question, which was: "Anthony, would you say that success in life and success in business come from the same attributes?"

Cracie answered: 'Leonora, we already have so much clear sightedness in common, I bet you can almost predict my answer. (I nodded, but I hadn't a clue.) Life and business are not just two goldfish swimming in the same bowl. They are two of the corporate predators of tomorrow. Why? Well, only they can see the sea beneath them, crack the glass with their X ray eyes and feast on the leftovers of their short sighted competitors"

I certainly recognised what a great intellect Ant, (as you know I came to call him), has. I'd bet that his MENSA rating is nearly as high as that of the female members of the Soculitherz family. I went on to ask him: "Are you in a long term relationship and, if so, with whom and for how long?" (I glanced down at the side pocket of Ant's brief case and I could just make out the title 'She Comes First' by Ian Kerner, so had high hopes for the evening.)

He answered that he wasn't, so we got off at Stevenage and spent a stimulating night together in Luton.

What I learned most from this first real talk with Ant was that 'Going it alone' will be a bit scary and you'll need to:

33. Approach all your early encounters with potential or first customers with an open mind. If they ask for anything that you can't immediately deliver, then negotiate some time to enable you to put it together.

I know entrepreneurs who have sourced new products, developed a brand new course, found an expert to partner them overnight and even invented a training school (they borrowed someone else's classroom) in order to meet what the customer wanted:

34. However uncomfortable you may feel, always push yourself into the action. Count yourself in to every piece of business that's going. It's a bit like 'You must buy a lottery ticket in order to win the lottery'.

FREEDOM from BOSSES FOREVER

35. Whatever help is on offer, especially free of charge from the public, private or third sector (charities, social enterprises and so forth), accept it – but, if you can, get help from someone that has started and run their own successful business. Starting your own business is no time to start thinking you know it all already – accept help.

Having cooled down from my meeting with Stephen I was then able to ring Ant to update him.

'Ant, I'm really not joining this Tochen network thing.'

'Were you asked to?'

'No but I'm sure that is just what young, serious Stephen's next step will be'

'Look babe, it really won't be. I'm certain they just want us to speak to the group in Madrid. It's worth it. Nice things happen to nice people who are in or work with the Tochen network. Why not just satisfy your curiosity and come with me? We'll have a great time.'

'What nice things?'

'Well, opportunities to win contracts or offers from folk with big houses on sunny islands to spend your vacation there.'

'Can they help me solve my assignment about politicians and fat cats getting rich while everything they touch goes bust?'

'Sure they can babe. Let's play Tochen. Have you got a daily paper with you? Pick a big story that fits with your assignment and I'll tell you if it sounds like a Tochen network thing.'

'Ok... it's the Malta Times; still not read it. One here about the ex boss of Royal Bank of Scotland, Sir Fred Goodwin, who is down for a £700,000 a year pension. Angry people and Prime Minister accused of 'sleeping on the job'. Letter from Sir Fred quoted to Lord thingy who was responsible for looking at all this stuff, said that he'd got an agreement with this Lord that he'd already given up enough. Government due to take action to stop it. Reading between the lines it looks like posturing on both sides, so there'll be a settlement with the Government claiming one over on the fat cats. Sir Fred will still end up with a fortune, but will appear peeved.

'Gotcha. That's almost certainly the Tochen network. If it defies reason or logic, or was something that needed fixing in the face of adverse public opinion, but no-one knows how it could be fixed, then it's probably the network and no-one will ever know how it's done.'

'What? Like the collapse of the twin towers looking like explosions, particularly building seven that wasn't hit, the Kelly suicide, the Hutton inquiry result, Enron, why no-one looked at the 258 congressmen accepting political contributions, Iran–Contra, Princess Diana, Ronald Reagan, Bill Clinton, George Bush, Camillagate, cash for honours, war on Iraq – all that stuff?'

'We'll never know but they can certainly help you with your assignment. Are you coming to Madrid?'

Chapter Six

How To Win Men and Affluent Friends

I want a man who only has to be kind and understanding. Is that too much to ask of a multi millionaire?

Zsa Zsa Gabor
Quoted in Quotable Quotes for Quoters by Aubrey Malone 2005

A few years ago now a BBC programme said there was one across-the-counter product that could help wrinkles disappear. That product cost about £17 and was available at Boots. Cue for a mad buying frenzy: women killing each other for a pot of the stuff and outrage that pots were selling on e-bay all over the world for five times the price.

My reason for telling you this? I get asked more questions about what can make you look young than I do about style. I really can't do with women in a state of denial about wanting to look young. Of course you do: you want the inside to match the outside. Get over feeling guilty about women who campaigned so that women shouldn't be judged by their looks and just take pride in looking how you want to look.

36. Looking good today isn't a statement that 'I've got good genes', it's saying 'that's what I choose to spend my time and money on' to feel good about myself. Your choice. No right and no wrong. We all should have a positive image of ourselves – not to compare to super celebrities, like me, but to feel OK inside and outside. If you want to do it, then do it.

If you need help to do it, then Leonora is here for you.

Tony Robinson OBE (with Soculitherz)

As you know, I have fond memories of Luton. It was in a hotel in Luton that I nearly imploded as a result of the frisson and fireworks achieved with motivational guru and fire walker, Ant Cracie. This time I was off to Luton airport accompanied by AC, as we had the opportunity to speak together for the very first time to a Tochen network group in Madrid.

I was looking forward to the 2 hour flight, as it would whisk me to a fantastic city where I'd soon be picking at tapas and quaffing Rioja with the beautiful people. It is a cultured, fashionable and classy place that parties through the night and it's perfect for my style, wit and elegance. The bad news is that, because our flight options are limited by our timetable, I'll be suffering silently, with baseball hat and dark glasses firmly on, from the indignity of flying there and back on Easy Jet.

On the flight out, I enjoyed teasing Ant with a few more 'So was that the Tochen network too?' Everything from UK&US Arms to Iraq, Halliburton Energy Services to the funnier ones like all the different versions of Bin Laden's death and how all the fines accumulated by the financial services, energy and food companies are just a small cost of doing business. But Ant did make me laugh when he explained that 'rubbish apologies' were a good indicator of Tochen members. It's because they meant to do the stuff, but, being Christians, they're not allowed to lie, so their apologies to people come out a little strange as in:

"I can apologise for the information that turned out to be wrong, but I can't, sincerely at least, apologise for removing Saddam." (Tony Blair on the dossier that led to war on Iraq)

"Mistakes have been made". (Ronald Reagan on the Iran–Contra scandal)

"I have expressed a degree of regret that could be equated with an apology." (Des Browne, UK Defence Secretary on hostages selling their stories)

FREEDOM from BOSSES FOREVER

"I misled people, including even my wife. I deeply regret that". (Bill Clinton on the Monica Lewinsky affair)

Madrid has also had a positive effect on my career. You will have read that it was in Madrid at a fashion awards show, where I was actually the first to open mouth kiss a top female model, which led to her losing her Coca Cola sponsorship.

Old Golden Balls, David Beckham, used to live there, but has never spoken to me since I interviewed that 'kiss and tell' model of a few years ago. Although my incisive journalism will remain unappreciated by his household, it nevertheless boosted my media career and the continued regular procreation by the posh one. The renewal of their marriage vows after 10 years seems to indicate that it did their relationship no harm either.

It was in Del Prado art gallery, whilst looking at a painting by my favourite big picture painter, Domenikos Theotokopoulos (you'd know him as the Greek – El Greco), when Anty Panty piped up with his 'network' theory. I was just commenting on how you could see the influence of Titian, whose stuff we'd seen earlier, and why he always put contemporary figures in his many religious works, with little regard for spatial depth, when Ant interrupted me. 'All these religious pictures remind me:

37. How important disciples were and how important it is that a new entrepreneur builds a support network quickly to help them through the early, vulnerable stages of their business'.

Zut! A problem with Ant is that, apart from when he's having sex, he's always thinking up bits for his stage show or books. This was not the place for me to drop my knickers, so I just had to let him continue.

Ant clearly had little interest in listening to my exposition of why El Greco was so suited to the late 16th and early 17th century religious fervour of Spain and how the unworldliness of much of his Mannerist painting always provided the perfect vehicle with which to express mystical events from the Bible. Instead, I had to listen to his theory on networking. So that we can move on, I've shortened it into three Leonorisms below.

38. The best way to learn what to do to be successful in your own enterprise is by doing things and learning from them.

Obvious isn't it? But although your business is unique, some of the mistakes you might make are not, so you must build a personal and business network from which you can learn in order to improve your chances of getting it right first time.

39. To set up your supportive network, you'll almost always include an individual or individuals who have already got the 'I run my own business' T shirt.

However, it can include a professional adviser – often this is an accountant – and a family member(s) or friend(s) to whom to turn for advice on how to solve business problems as they arise. A previous boss or work colleague(s) from whose skills you feel you can learn, is good too. Of course, add in any people (e.g. book keeper; web maintenance) you're paying to take on tasks that prevent you from doing what you need to do.

40. This network will give you the vital support, learning and confidence to succeed in the first, vital, eighteen months.

If a prospective entrepreneur has the right support, it can improve the chances of surviving 3 years by a minimum of 20% and often more than double their chances of success. I've suggested to your Brit government that anyone without a job who wants to start a business should have a voucher to cash in for 8 weeks training and support from a private sector advice professional and small business owner, such as an accountant, and have their first year's subscription to an approved business network or club paid for by the Government.

FREEDOM from BOSSES FOREVER

This would be much more cost effective and productive for individuals and the country than all their other unemployment into employment measures which, as usual, rely on giving all the support money to the bigger companies, most of whom have been in decline for the last twenty years.

Currently the Government has two main initiatives: £1 billion for training low skilled employees and another £1.2 billion for apprenticeships. Big Mac - McDonalds - is the biggest beneficiary of these funds with 10,000 apprentices, followed by the big construction, car and utilities companies. No surprises there then.

Now, let me tell you about our flamenco evening which followed our pretty successful first presentation as a duo. It's a wonder I remember anything, as we drank a riverful of Rioja and ate tapas of whole little fish with their eyes staring at me, which combined to make me feel very queasy. Nevertheless the renowned Soculitherz family constitution saw me through and I witnessed an amazing display of flamenco.

The combination of voice (2 lead singers), guitar (2 guitarists – one a 6'6" god), dance (2 women and one rather effeminate man), and percussion (everyone clapping and clicking fingers) created a magnificently expressive musical and visual spectacle.

Some sequences were traditional and very close to its Southern Spanish gypsy roots, but some were very contemporary. The final dance by the younger, taller and leaner woman was outstanding, as she developed the co-ordinating sinuous arm and hand gestures with intricate heelwork. The rhythm (compas) and emotional motivation (duende) was wonderfully set up for the dance and we experienced the full range of emotions from frivolity to sorrow (we'd had the gay in the previous dance!).

It is so sad that an evening of high art can be brought crashing down by AC's dumb comment that 'they must have forgotten their castanets'

The next morning in Madrid we attended a small, private meeting of Tochen entrepreneurs and I was able to ask on your behalf, dear reader: "what are the important abilities one needs to start a business successfully?"

It was acknowledged that, in many countries, what stops people quitting the rat race to control their own destiny in their own business is fear or lack of confidence. One fear is that they do not have the necessary abilities to start a business successfully. What abilities do they need? Well, we've packed all these into Leonorisms throughout 'Stripping for Freedom' by Leonora Soculitherz.

After returning to our hotel to check out, a colleague told us that we didn't need to worry about excess baggage surcharges when AC and I checked in for more delights from Easy Jet. This is because AC had been the successful target of thieves, who had stolen his laptop bag. Along with the bag were the contents of laptop, mobile phone, memory sticks, pens, files and all sorts of valuable personal and business items.

It had been a classy theft in just 90 seconds as they substituted an empty black bag for the one they took and managed to fool our fellow conference delegates and four reception staff, who all had a clear view of proceedings.

AC was in obvious discomfort about his life's work disappearing. More so, because we knew their theft was not about developing their entrepreneurial skills by reading AC's writing. What the gang bosses will have been most interested in is the data on people and organisations. Fortunately, AC is ready for these days and only saves sensitive data to his password controlled digital vault. This puts him light years ahead of the UK Government which collects more data on UK individuals than any other country, but then leaves the data on buses, trains and in supermarkets.

AC says that collecting data is a Tochen network imperative, so one should never think that it's an accident when personal data is left everywhere. It's a way of ensuring that no questions are asked of the

Government when someone uses the data in a way that wouldn't be appropriate for the Government to do. Oh well!

Nevertheless, the Spanish gang bosses will have been upset they didn't get what they wanted. My vision is of a scene written by Cervantes, with a backdrop of fighting windmills, where an angry Spaniard in pirate's garb with one eye, one leg, a parrot on his shoulder and bandaged fingers is seen hurling the offending bag and all its contents into the Manzaneres river.

The Leonorism is:

41. Always back up your data in a different and secure place. Most people choose that place to be in the cloud to assist working from many different locations. Losing data can kill your new enterprise and insurance will never cover your loss.

I'm not keen on generalisations about differences between the sexes, although I've always thought that Coco Chanel – "As long as you know most men are like children, you know everything" – and Cher – "The trouble with some women is they get all excited about nothing and then they marry him" – made some pretty good generalisations.

However, for the sake of providing good advice on what it will take to strip for freedom and run your own business, there are definitely some valuable real life and business lessons that you can learn from looking at successful women entrepreneurs:

42. Selflessness, focus, productivity and belief are the positive traits that I would have you copy.

I hate stereotyping but there is a bit of Venus and Mars in all this. The strength of many men is that they will often exploit opportunities and take risks, whilst many women entrepreneurs may be more risk averse. However, many men have the Achilles heel of ego and status needs. It often leads to a lack of pragmatism and an unwillingness to compromise and the financial crash.

Men will declare war on real or imagined opponents, not because there is any point to it, but because they've got the bombs to do it and think they might look weak by not doing the bombing. Women entrepreneurs are often more selfless and, as such, not as prone to: the need to be loved; the need to be admired for their status; the trappings of status (type/mode of: car, travel, office, club, event/meals, toys/gadgets); and the need to be the centre of attention.

Many women find it easier to separate business wants, feelings and behaviours from personal, domestic and leisure interests and responsibilities:

43. Finding some degree of separation of business and personal lives is to be recommended for everyone. Your business persona has to be harder to cope with rejection or people taking advantage of you. Your business persona can remain focused.

Recognising that 'it's only business' and that business arrangements and alliances can be made to work, whatever the sacrifices in personal esteem terms, are good attitudes with which to start your business. Women are often more:

44. Willing to take advice and training to achieve the aims on which they're focused and will carefully build a trusted support network.

Once they have enough confidence in their business idea, many successful women entrepreneurs will stay focused on making it work, whereas many male executives and professionals who go it alone are not as successful, because they get distracted too quickly into seeking out wherever they think the grass may be greener.

This strong focus ('they just get on with it') which many women entrepreneurs share, definitely leads to smart working. Women often have to balance more non-business responsibilities and therefore use business time better:

45. They are often very productive in meeting the business needs during the working hours they have allocated for that day.

They don't have such a need to be seen (or even to play during working hours) and, as such, can 'job and finish' and keep their business moving forward step by step. If they also rely on others, then this clarity of focus and direction will gain high commitment and productivity from staff and suppliers. All of this builds belief that they can succeed and belief in their product or service:

46. Belief and passion for what you do transmits itself to new and existing customers. It makes business building through credible selling and high quality of supply much easier. Doing what you know and love is important.

Was Athene (a Goddess, of course) the first major entrepreneur? This talk of Achilles' heel – the only exposed bit for Paris to shoot at – reminds me what a moody sod Achilles was, much like many of the high status male bosses I've seen fail in their own businesses. It all started with him sulkily staying in his tent and not fighting the Trojans, because he was peeved that the gods had taken away his favourite toy (a slave girl). Then, when he came back, he was still pretty petulant, what with all that dragging Hector's corpse round and round the city walls.

This was despite all Goddess Athene's help and wise, strategic interventions in the Trojan wars. In fact, to succeed as an entrepreneur one would be well served to get in the zone of Athene, the Goddess of Wisdom. Athene may have been the very first role model entrepreneur too, as she developed one of the world's most successful enterprises when she stamped her foot and gave rise to the first olive tree in history.

Greece has always fascinated the Soculitherz family. Looking at Europe from as far away as Canada, it's interesting to see how the sophistication of the UK civil service/government machine keeps students and citizens in check or, as some Greek political philosophers have said, 'depressed', whereas in Greece there is the worst civil unrest in Europe for 40 years.

The world outrage over Iraq in 2003 never abated in Greece. In England, however, I remember watching Sir Alan Ayckbourn interview Sir Harold Pinter, in the Stephen Joseph Theatre in Scarborough. He'd just presented his anti-Iraq war/anti-America poetry and there was just a collective 'Oh Well' frustration throughout the audience, that 'we demonstrated, but there's nothing we can really do'.

However in Greece the students and others decided to say 'No' to politicians just being in power for power itself. It may never affect the UK because of its special relationship with the US, but this Marlborough Lite smoking, female fashion journalist, with admittedly little political nous, wouldn't be surprised if the Greek sentiments spread across the rest of Europe. Maybe that's why Governments are getting so cute about collecting personal data.

Certainly, women entrepreneurs like the Goddess Athene, do not try to copy male characteristics. They remain feminine. PG Wodehouse, through the words of Bertram Wooster, explains the difference between the feminine traits which I've described as being good for an entrepreneur and the squashy soupiness that is not good. Here, Wooster describes Madeline Bassett to whom he, assisted by Jeeves, is constantly trying to avoid becoming betrothed:

"I can well imagine that a casual observer, if I had confided to him my qualms at the idea of being married to this girl, would have raised his eyebrows and been at a loss to understand, for she was undeniably an eyeful, being slim, svelte and bountifully equipped with golden hair and all the fixings. But where the casual observer would have been making his bloomer was in overlooking that squashy soupiness of hers, that subtle air she had of being on the point of talking baby talk. She was the sort of girl who puts her hands over a husband's eyes, as he is crawling in to breakfast with a morning head and says 'Guess Who?'"

FREEDOM from BOSSES FOREVER

I wondered if Ant was beginning to think I was a bit squashy soupy in my reaction to Tochen. On the way back from Madrid we had one of those arguments that it's probably better to participate in than to have to watch. It started OK as we'd had a good time at the event and I agreed there were some very nice people there.

I didn't even mind him drawing 4 x 4 circles on my napkin and he made me laugh when he said Mrs Clinton, Mrs Major, Mrs Archer and Mrs Prescott all stayed with their husbands after the 'indiscretions' because they were in the Women's branch of Tochen.

But then it just got silly and I started to think he wanted me to say that I'd like to join. In the end I went over the top and said I thought the Tochen network was 'discriminatory against women, faith and small business owners'. I said it was just 'secret society and boys' games stuff that has been going on for centuries'. It made it even worse because I'd found out that their accessories (watches, cufflinks etc) were modified and were different types of communications gadgets.

Anyway, Ant said he'd keep to his promise of getting me some key interviews for my assignment and I stopped winding him up. He really looked as if he might explode. I amaze myself sometimes at how long and persistently I can turn the screw.

Tony Robinson OBE (with Soculitherz)

Chapter Seven

The 'M' myth

There are girls, few perhaps but to be found if one searches carefully, who when their advice is ignored and disaster ensues, do not say 'I told you so'. Mavis was not of their number.

PG Wodehouse
From Pearls, Girls and Monty Bodkin, Chapter 11.

No style tips to start with here, because this is the big interview chapter. Well, just one then: in a recession you'll see lots of stuff about thrift rather than chic. Believe me, a recession is your opportunity to be chic for less.

Before I tell you about my interviews and the outstanding tips I gathered from these really good people of whom you will never have heard, I just want to share with you an e-mail I got, whilst in Madrid, from my inept and clueless agent, Tony Robinson OBE.

A word of explanation; TR is not only a hopeless agent, an uncoordinated danger (to hair and frocks) at dinners, parties and receptions but he is also a past master at mangling the English language. I'm sure that no-one has understood what he's said for years.

This makes it all the stranger that he acts as a consultant to Oxbridge educated, well dressed, London based, senior executives and civil servants. I've always suspected that they write his reports and recommendations to themselves and of course he's dirt cheap – enough money for a cinder toffee ice cream and a pint of Black Sheep and he's anybody's.

FREEDOM from BOSSES FOREVER

Talking of sheep that is why he wrote to me. He was seeking my advice. Why he expects to me know anything about sheep puzzles me but my best guess is that he confuses Canadians, like me, with New Zealanders. He will never visit either place, has no spatial awareness and a pathetic grasp of what inhabits planet earth. Therefore, it is unlikely he will appreciate that there is a difference in size between the two countries, some distance between them and that the Arctic polar bear is unlikely to be found in Christchurch or the kiwi in Toronto.

The reason he was seeking my advice on sheep is that he has set up a 'School for Entrepreneurial Sheep' near Goathland (he probably thought this sounded appropriate) on the North Yorkshire Moors. How he came to win this government funded contract to train enterprise skills and know how to sheep may be surprising to you but it is not surprising to me.

Apparently some government departments had an underspend (amazing really after all the £billions they've used up supporting big companies in handouts, training grants and the City of London Benevolence Fund). The priorities like expense/allowance claims, second homes, pensions, city bonuses, ex Ministers' top 500 consultancies, regime change, media and food fraud damage limitation inquiries had all been dealt with and so some speculative new programmes could now be funded.

TR had been to see them about enterprise apprenticeships in the land-based industries. I suspect he'd been interested in farmers' sons and daughters setting up micro-breweries but as usual his inability to speak English completely confused his potential clients. What he left the meeting with was a short term contract, to be completed this financial year, to pilot an enterprise academy for farm animals, starting with sheep.

Apparently, when TR had, probably hopefully, thrown the words 'supply chain' into the conversation the civil servants thought he'd come up with a novel idea of a reverse supply chain.

Tony Robinson OBE (with Soculitherz)

Simply put this would get the animals which provide the end products (wool, beef, bacon, milk, eggs, turkey) to gain more entrepreneurial skills and then teach these skills up line to the farmer, and the farmer to the abattoir manager, and so on, eventually reaching the Tesco and McDonalds directors and finally Government Ministers.

Who would know more about innovation, risk taking, increasing productivity and better value for money for customers than the animal itself? Here's TR's e-mail to me:

A School – somewhere in North Yorkshire – Thursday.

Dear Leonora,

My first sheeprentices have arrived but I'm not convinced they quite have the right attitude for entrepreneurship – sheepish isn't the kind of outgoing behaviour we were looking for. The little lambs seem to have more get up and go – but they've gone and I don't know where. Anyway, any advice you can give would be welcome as Ofsted, a government body, are inspecting in a week's time. Hopefully, by then, my sheeprentices will have at least learned to sit still at their desks.

They look startled all the time – is that normal? They seem to only know the first two letters of the alphabet and in the reverse order. It's going to be a long job to get them ready to do their pitch on Dragons' Den and I'm not even going to mention the word dragon at this stage. Lord Sugar will be a bit frustrated with them, on his show, as even when you split them up into different teams they all go off together and intermingle. No obvious leaders up to now.

I've taken the advice of a local farmer to try to keep them in line with the threat of mint sauce and a salsa dip but as I can't understand much of his Yorkshire accent, this far North in Yorkshire, I've no idea why. I don't think my dream of becoming the Farm Animal Enterprise Tsar is going to happen. My brief was a bit woolly from the start and I wasn't sure about the Local Enterprise Partnership's diagnostic to select the candidates.

Any help will be greatly appreciated

FREEDOM from BOSSES FOREVER

Your faithful, and honoured, literary agent,

Tony Robinson OBE

I hope you can see why I will never collaborate again with this fool on a business book or anything.

OK so let's get on with the big interviews. The only thing which is a bit confusing is that all the five interviewees have similar names. There's Michel, Michelle, Michaela, Michael and Michaela again. I can't change their names just to make it less confusing can I?

I'm sure you've been following my travels, but as a reminder I'm on my way back to Scarborough from Luton airport, after having had an interesting two days in Madrid. In a couple of days' time I'll be escaping to London and there I aim to complete my assignment within three weeks max. So no more North Yorkshire or Tony Robinson very soon. Sad, I know.

Stranded at York station for 45 minutes awaiting my connection, I found a corner of Costa Coffee and sat with my back to the centre to avoid celebrity stalkers and autograph hunters. I was able to drink my skinny latte undisturbed and substantially review one of W H Smith's current, top selling books for budding entrepreneurs, 'The Millionaire Upgrade'.

It tells the story of a young executive wimp who ends up getting a first class upgrade which puts him in the best seat on the plane next to a millionaire entrepreneur. Throughout the flight the millionaire business man, whose dress and writing implements mark him as a man of distinction and a bore, mentors his new companion. He gives him the secrets to his success. The book is apparently based on interviews with 50 successful entrepreneurs and a similar, fortunate, in flight conversation with Britain's entrepreneurial hero, Richard Branson.

The fictitious millionaire entrepreneur (not Richard Branson) regularly uses the words 'I believe'. I BELIEVE turns out to be a mnemonic for all the things you need to do to be mega successful. It's a pretty dodgy, lazy type of mnemonic too as the 'V' stands for 'Very, Very' something or other.

Anyway, by the time I finally got to Malton I'd speed read and equally speedily discarded the 'Millionaire Upgrade.' It's a bit like eating a Snickers bar: you get a quick high followed by a stodgy, guilt-ridden low. It's well meaning but ultimately an impractical 'Stay focused, stay cool and get rich with the right attitude and network' type tract.

But, considering my earlier reading matter, the spooky part came next. At Malton, a very elderly, shabbily dressed, unshaven drunk boarded the train and sat next to me. I should explain that, as usual and as befits my status I am sitting in the first class compartment. My new companion would probably not have a first class ticket but, as stated earlier, this is not unusual on the utterly misnamed Trans-Pennine Express.

It is likely that in this full carriage of would-be town criers I was the only one with a first class ticket. Anyway, when the conductor asked to see our tickets, my companion asked for "un billet simple pour Scarborough". I instantly warmed to my new travel companion and explained to the bemused conductor that all he'd asked for was a single to Scarborough.

French is my favourite language, but I realise that it is as great a mystery to the English as the delights of Scarborough Football Club's 'pie and peas' are to me. So I'll recount in English the gist of my conversation with my new best, ex-legionnaire friend.

Michel served with distinction in the French Foreign Legion, but he left me under no illusions about just how tough it was. He reminisced about once being last in line of three very sick soldiers who were asked to stand by their hospital beds whilst their resolve was tested by their commanding officer:

'What's your problem legionnaire?' '

FREEDOM from BOSSES FOREVER

'Chronic syphilis, sir' says the legionnaire.

'What treatment are you getting?' asks the officer.

'Five minutes with the wire brush each day, sir' says the legionnaire.

'What's your ambition legionnaire?'

'To get back to the front line, sir.'

'Good man,' says the officer and goes to the next in line, 'What's your problem legionnaire?'

'Chronic piles, sir' comes the reply.

'What treatment are you getting?' asks the officer.

'Five minutes with the wire brush each day, sir' says the second legionnaire.

'And what's your ambition?'

'To get back to the front, sir.'

'Good man,' says the officer and finally approaches Michel, standing by the next bed.

'And what's your problem legionnaire?'

'Chronic gum disease' replies Michel.

'What is your treatment, legionnaire?'

'Five minutes with the wire brush each day, sir' says Michel.

'And what's your ambition, legionnaire?'

'To get the wire brush before the other two, sir' replies Michel.

Michel chuckled at the end of this tall tale, but it was one he probably now believed. I'm sure the joint effect of a memory being shot to pieces over a long lifetime and the booze leads to many people, like Michel, believing what they dreamed or have been told has actually happened to them.

However, there was no doubting him when he told me his riches to rags story. After returning to civilian life Michel started his own confectionery business in Paris. Through innovation, hard work and recruitment of a brilliant chocolatier, the business grew from one shop with a small preparation room to a multi million business, operating from a small factory, with 12 shops throughout France.

Eighteen years ago he sold his successful business to enjoy the fruits of his labour and travel the world. One day on a flight back to Paris from Singapore, he got talking to a young American business woman and heiress who, to cut a long story short, persuaded him to invest in her hotel and leisure business. The business grew, as did their relationship and they married and had children.

Eight years ago Michel began a long relationship with a famous French actress. Whilst a French man having a mistress is, regrettably, nothing new, especially amongst politicians and the bourgeoisie, it was unpardonable to his young wife, who promptly divorced him. This was just three years ago. She was also responsible for having him sued for various anti-competitive practices to do with introducing infectious diseases into other hotels (ironically, including some in Scarborough). This all spelled rack and ruin for Michel.

Even though he told the tale beautifully in French, I got pretty fed up with Michel, his story and his halitosis. Yet, remembering 'the Millionaire Upgrade' I did ask him if he had a mnemonic which my dear readers, my fellow strippers for freedom, could use to help them to the level of entrepreneurial success that he'd had before he let his 'lunch box', as you say, become his Achilles heel. La Clef, the key, is what he gave me, for what it's worth (and it is a lot of Leonorisms):

47. Luck – you make your own

FREEDOM from BOSSES FOREVER

48. Application – breeds opportunities

49. Commitment – overcomes failure

50. Leadership – by example

51. Enthusiasm – you can never have too much of it

52. Feu – (French word for fire) – in your belly

Here's my write up of the first of the big interviews I did for you. This one was with Michelle and Michaela, a few days ago, at Luton airport. They were obliging enough to meet me there so that I could give you the benefit of their excellent advice on promotion and public relations. Michelle and Michaela are an item.

I watch Michelle, with her worn-high, honey-blonde hair in a side-swept fringe and her wine glass crooked coolly in her finger as she gesticulates to emphasise each point. If I were to turn it would definitely be for someone like Michelle. The lesbian fling or even long term relationship doesn't raise an eyebrow anymore, as we know that a quarter of all women's bedroom fantasies involve having sex with another woman.

Trouble is that everything I read about the advantages for hopping over to the Sapphic side of the fence seem to be about 'Men are so crap in bed, aren't they?' I haven't found this to be altogether true. Anyway, it is still one of the UK's big talking points that the advertising campaign for which Michelle and Michaela are famous was 'Meanings in the Mornings'.

Michelle Strongbone and Michaela Rock are the co-founders and co-owners of Fabsolutely2Good plc. Fabsolutely2Good plc's brilliant 'Meanings in the Mornings' campaign, which owed everything to Michelle and Michaela's drop dead creative excellence, now appears as a case study in the Chartered Institute of Marketing examination papers.

Tony Robinson OBE (with Soculitherz)

In essence, their assignment, a few years ago now, was to turn a breakfast cereal called 'Good and Chunky', full of nutritional goodness, but extremely short on palatability, into a best seller. This they have more than achieved with the breakfast experience we know today as 'Meanings in the Mornings.' Clever packaging, which works so well with the new name they gave to the cereal, is an essential element of the integrated marketing solution.

The 'Meanings in the Mornings' carton is oversized and completely black, both inside and out. On opening the pack, consumers find a small gold disc asking them to 'Hold the carton above your head and look carefully inside for the answer to the question "What's it all about?" This 'Meanings' question changes monthly. Those who think they have the answer can telephone, text, e-mail or go straight online to the website to log in their answer.

Each month one hundred lucky winners can choose between detox. and pilates weekends at health spas throughout Europe, or the more popular ten minute 'shop for choc until you drop' at Tesco. The TV and radio advertising campaign builds brand value by linking 'Meanings' to feelings of heightened sexual arousal.

The television ad. shows scantily clad Becks and J-Lo look-alikes crunching happily on their 'Meanings'. They switch on their Roberts digital radio and Robbie Williams's "Let me entertain you" is heard.

Slowly the couple slip from view under the breakfast table. The camera focuses on a close up shot of the black 'Meanings in the Mornings' carton. (Incidentally, the same carton was used in the kitchen scene early on in Tarrantino's 'Kill Bill Vol 1'). To the sound of Robbie Williams and suggestive noises from beneath the table, we now focus on a puff of white smoke coming out of the top of the black carton. Superimposed on the white smoke we see the slogan *'Meanings in the Mornings – so good it's wicked!'*

The Fabsolutely2Good agency nicknamed the ad. 'Robbie for Pope!' and it hasn't done the singer's popularity any harm at all. The ad. doesn't work quite as well on radio, but the fun element of putting the black box over your head has now become a celebrity trend, with many using the box instead of sunglasses.

Michelle and Michaela even leaked to me that some celebrities have insisted all their bodyguards and minders wear the cartons 24/7. They are helped in their surveillance work by images and tracking data relayed to them on a small screen from an overhead helicopter and earphones inside each carton.

Anyway, whilst gathering this awesome intelligence for all you 'strippers for freedom' it didn't stop me asking Michaela: 'What's so good about a lesbian relationship?' After her reply 'Multiple orgasms, no wet spot and…', I shut her up by saying we'd better get on with their tips to help you promote your new business. Here are Michelle and Michaela of Fabsolutely2Good plc's top 10 tips:

53. Aim beyond what you think you are capable of. Put it in words (copy) first and design and images second. (e.g. "I want to be as famous as Persil Automatic" – Victoria Beckham.)

54. Promote the positive and diminish the negative. Take the basic truth in your idea and bring it to life in words and images.

55. Link your messages to your clients'/ customers' wants, but don't oversell what you can do for them. They must trust your promise and it is far better to give them more than they expected.

56. Remember that business promotion is show business, so don't be afraid to take some risks to 'entertain'. Use novel ideas to give you an edge. You must 'put on a show' in copy, on the web, on stage and with press interviews.

57. Think through the problem you can solve for your clients through your copy. Produce it in short sentences and short paragraphs. Plain English is good too.

58. Link to 5 above, by your simple, attention-getting headline or slogan. For example, 'Bad news for Dads' as a heading to show how few companies are encouraging paternity leave.

59. Short press releases with an interesting photo/image get into the press more often. For example, an April Fool release with a photo of the business owners superimposed in eggs in an egg cup with the heading 'No yolking' and the following story:

> "Hard on the heels of burgers and baked potatoes, comes what a city firm hopes will be the next fast food fad – boiled eggs. Opening on Monday in Central Milton Keynes, Egg-U-Fill will offer more than 200 exotic fillings for hard and soft eggs, ranging from traditional sea salted chips and jelly to rum flavoured beetroot, claims Managing Director, Ed Curry. But providing the restaurant's giant egg cup centrepiece meant a scramble for the Newport Pagnell-based Business Advisory Bureau. 'We are certain that Egg-U-Fill will poach some of the fast food market share and put Milton Keynes on the map,' said BAB's Clare Francis."

60. With business-to-business services, the objective of your direct marketing copy will often be to get delegates to an event, seminar or meeting.

61. Don't forget to get in a really good 'call to action' and don't be afraid to repeat it in your copy.

62. 90% of the inspiration for copy for advertising, direct mailers, web pages and press releases comes from other adverts, web pages, direct mailers and press releases. So copy what works; for example, one successful direct mailer for a software supplier was really just a copy of a successful mailer for garden tools.

Before I left Michelle and Michaela I asked for some personal advice. I explained I was thinking of taking on an agent and didn't think I could afford Max Clifford, so what did they think about TR? I wasn't sure whether: "Badly bearded and badly dressed, but you know that", and "let's say conscientious but not cautious" was good or bad.

FREEDOM from BOSSES FOREVER

I also asked if they'd heard of the Tochen network and whether they thought that Government and media do work together on the big issues like Scargill and the Miners' Strike, where the NUM was clearly right, but Scargill and the miners were vilified or, more recently, Iraq? I added that no newspaper proprietor had ever put pressure on me. They just said 'Yes' and 'Yes'. For people who deal in words, they don't seem to know too many sometimes, but overall I think they've given good value to you, my fellow strippers for freedom.

Next stop was Darren and Debbie's excellent Café Del Mar at the seafront in Scarborough's North Bay. Darren and Debbie are serial entrepreneurs, but over many years they've proved with Café Del Mar that a great effort, a great hunch, a great location and great choice in contemporary snack food and drink are a winning formula, even in a recession.

However I wasn't there to interview Darren and Debbie but Sir Michael Graysting, a very senior ex civil servant, who has retired to a village in the North Yorkshire moors. Although he is in his mid to late fifties he has put together a portfolio of enterprises which are proving successful. So unusual was his story and so important is it to give my more senior strippers for freedom hope of success, (and I might also discover something to solve my mystery assignment), that I just had to interview him. AC and TR fixed it up for me.

I'd heard Sir Michael could be quite prickly to deal with, so although I don't usually buy my interviewees a gift, I bought him a Jake 'The Snake' wrestling figure, a packet of Bridlington's finest John Bull cinder toffee and a baseball hat with a Yorkshire Rose on it from the tourist shop on the Scarborough front.

He said 'Very kind' to my gifts, and in answer to my question as to whether he'd wear the hat said: '"I might whilst gardening"'. So, with confidence boosted I asked: 'Have you heard of the Tochen network and do you think they're behind the decision not to help small business owners but ensure the failed fat cats get richer?'. He said he hadn't come to talk about such things and made to leave even before he'd sat down.

'Sorry Sir Michael. I promise that I just want to find out about your own enterprises after leaving the Civil Service. Please sit down and let me buy you a coffee". "I'll have a pot of tea, please".

Sir Michael couldn't hear the 'Phew' as I strode away to get his order, but it was one mightily relieved fashion-come-investigative journalist who ordered a pot of tea and a black coffee with a double vodka shot in it.

Returning to the table, I started again:

'Sir Michael, my book is about what it takes to go it alone in your own enterprise. Your advice would be particularly welcome for the many, shall we say, more mature people who have held very senior positions but are now looking to do their own thing. What made you decide to pursue your enterprising interests? (I didn't add 'even though you've got a big fat civil service pension and never need work again').

'Well, Ms Soculitherz, it was partly that I felt too young to be retired, partly that I had the opportunity and probably, mainly, that I wanted to prove to myself that I could stand on my own two feet, as it were"

'What were the opportunities?'

'Well I had a number of Oxford chums in the media – in television particularly – and knowing of my interest in snakes, one of them asked whether I'd present a wildlife programme with some links to the tourism regrowth after the tsunami, in Sri Lanka.'

'And did that lead to you writing your children's books featuring 'Sammy and Sandra Snake?'

'Well partly. Mainly it arose from my grandson's eagerness for my bedtime stories that started me thinking more children might enjoy them. As you know, they usually have a bit of a moral message in them, so parents seem all in favour.'

FREEDOM from BOSSES FOREVER

'And the success of that led to you develop management training techniques based on snake charming?'

'Ho, Ho (he sort of laughed), not at all, not at all..... that was the PM's idea: he'd always wanted me to pass on my experience to fast track civil servants at the Civil Service College. He was rather taken with the story about why Malta has snakes, but no poisonous snakes. Do you know it?'

I confessed I did, having recently been in Malta. He looked disappointed. I said it was to do with St Paul, shipwrecked, spending a few months there, and being bitten by a snake, after which there were no more poisonous snakes.

'Yes, that'll do', he said. "Well, the PM thought we should teach the civil service leaders of the future how to spot and neutralise people in key public service positions who might be inclined to become 'snakes in the grass'.

'Neutralise?'

'Influence them to act in the better interests of the public good and country.'

'What happens if you can't influence them?'

'Well usually we can – certainly after my training – but if that fails then we have ways of diminishing their influence.'

'Such as?'

'I'm not going there Ms Soculitherz, but you will notice that people who are really going against policy often lose their credibility and then their posts. We don't need to put anything in the water supply you know, they are just shown up as being past their sell by date. They become an embarrassment and their views become 'no longer relevant'. Next question, on my current interests please.'

I thought I'd wrap it up by giving Sir Michael the floor, as it were. 'Well finally, Sir Michael, as you're now a TV presenter, writer and consultant/ trainer, perhaps I could just turn on my recorder and you could give my prospective readers your tips on 'going it alone'. This is what Sir Michael said, and very useful it is too, methinks:

'Certainly. Well it is a bit of a jungle out there, so here are three tips on some animals to avoid, some to befriend and some to emulate:

63. Never attempt to charm the snakes (Leonora here: snakes alive – well that's a surprise then!) **In the lead up to starting your business and during the first year in business you'll encounter more snakes and scorpions than in the rest of your entrepreneurial lifespan.**

Many snakes and scorpions look friendly as they seem to promise you 'possible' work. They offer training, consultancy and advice to help you succeed. They can supply you with all sorts of business efficiency aids. They can make both you and your new business look good by supplying vehicles, premises, technology, print, media and advertising. You're easy prey and vulnerable.

They speak with forked tongue and will sting you. Their venom is not only poisonous to your financial well being, it depletes your energy levels, blurs your focus and bloats you up with stuff you don't need. This all eats away at the time you should be spending with prospective customers.

So, make a list of the people you need to charm and suppliers you really must deal with and don't try and charm the rest. Learn to say: 'No, I haven't got the time right now. Thank you and goodbye'.

64. Be cautious about surrounding yourself with cheeky monkeys. Some of the cute monkeys around you will also pickpocket your time and morale. They'll find reasons why things can't be done or won't work. Worse, they'll waste your time by getting you to play games – the kind of games that the rats in the rat race play.

These games stop you doing the things that are the lifeblood for starting and initially running your business. Their games include: 'Endless, pointless meetings'; 'Visions, strategies, plans and charts'; 'Systems, processes, standards and management controls'; and 'Rules, regulations and human resource management'. Watch out for prefixes or synonyms such as 'Ongoing, zero sum, one-stop, outcome, paradigm, radar, reality check, quality, game plan and low hanging fruit'. Whatever these terms relate to will be rubbish. If you see any monkeys with 'reasons why not' or 'corporate games', then either cage them or send them to your competitors.

A few of the monkeys will be friendly, supportive and fun to be with. They'll pickpocket ideas and practices from your competitors that will work for you. They'll find ways of climbing or swinging over obstacles. Above all, they'll make you laugh and keep you going through the long hours you'll need to work. Surround yourself with these cheeky monkeys.

65. Learn from the dominant lion. The people from whom you should learn are those who have achieved something similar to what you want to achieve. There is a lifestyle in the jungle of which I naturally disapprove, but I've been informed that it's a lifestyle from which aspiring male and female entrepreneurs should learn.

This unlikely role model is the dominant male lion. Successful entrepreneurs are often disliked because of their continual hunger for more success. Success breeds success. Everything that is sacrificed and all the long hours worked are worth it in order to 'make the kill' of gaining enough profitable work to ensure future success.

Often the ultimate aim of the prospective entrepreneur is to reach the same position, within a couple of years, as the dominant male in a pride of lions. Once you're the dominant lion it is the rest of the pride that does the work to get the kill. You get the best share of the meals, all the sex and get to do all the serious roaring.

Finally, my last case in this chapter of wonderful entrepreneurs of whom you've never heard, is about Mickey. Mickey is my favourite girlfriend in England. I met Michaela Shear-Dawson, (Mickey to me), on my first Scarborough visit. Although not a celebrity, Mickey is well known in the business world, as she has won many entrepreneur awards:

66. Go for every award going; fantastic publicity and sometimes prizes too.

Mickey's award winning business is called www.share-alodge-room.com.

Like all great business ideas it is a simple idea, which takes a proven format into a new sector. Realising the success of internet-based businesses which put people together, (such as dating services, 'Friends Reunited'), and share-a-car type sites, along with sales agencies such as 'TopTable.com', which sells restaurant tables, Mickey just put these proven formulae together in her www.share-a-lodge-room.com.

Mickey saw a business opportunity in the fact that most Travel Lodges, IBIS, Premier Inns, Days Inns and the like charge accommodation by the room, not by the person. Her website provides the opportunity for someone about to stay in a lodge-type room to contact other members through the website and see if 1 or 2 additional people want to share that room. This not only reduces each person's cost by half/two thirds, it can lead to romantic liaisons as a bonus.

It's closer to bed dating than speed dating, although by all reports it's amazing how fast things can happen. Membership is just £5 a month, so you don't have to be a regular traveller or dater to get your money's worth. It doesn't need advertising because everyone loves a bargain, with the possibility of a new friendship or more as a bonus. Good news like this travels fast.

Another of Mickey's nifty ideas was a way of ensuring all her members behaved themselves. As part of their welcome pack each member gets a 'share a room' best practice guidelines booklet. They also get a battery powered bracelet. The bracelet must be worn at all

FREEDOM from BOSSES FOREVER

times in the room as a condition of membership. It has a traffic light system on it.

As the new room mates get to know each other, they can see the reaction they're getting by looking at their roommate's bracelet. A red light always means no touching and not interested. Orange means no touching but could be interested. Green means proceed with circumspect touching. Naturally at any time the lights can switch back from green to red and then it's hands off again. The system isn't foolproof, as those who are colour blind or just indecisive can have a fairly frantic night.

Just like e-bay and Amazon, members are also rated against various criteria and this information appears against their name on the website. However, unlike e-bay or Amazon some members choose to room with people with low rather than high ratings.

As most of my discerning and admiring readers know, I have long dark brown hair with a dark purple highlight. Mickey has blonde hair and despite it being naturally blonde, it was only after becoming a dot.com millionaire with 'bargainbonk.com' – as it's known in the trade – that Mickey was taken seriously in the business world.

I'm not altogether sure about whether conferences aimed solely at women entrepreneurs are a good idea or not. It can lead to distancing from an inclusive business world, greater stereotyping, bitchiness and a severe shoe bill. Introduce a man into the conference, either as a speaker or entertainer, and strange things can happen to them as they realise they're alone with 500 positive, strong and successful women.

At the Blackpool Hilton, just a few weeks ago where Mickey was winning another award, this time for her business contribution to the environment (savings on hotel heating), there was a perfect example of the parallel world created at women entrepreneur conferences.

The after dinner entertainment was provided by a ventriloquist. Nearly 80% of the audience were blondes, but as I've said strange things happen to men in this environment. He clearly thought 'blonde' jokes would go down well. He was an excellent ventriloquist with a traditional cheeky chappie doll, but after 15 or more consecutive blonde gags, he was becoming very irksome.

After the 'Why don't blondes work as lift attendants? They can't remember the route', followed by 'Why couldn't the blonde write the number 11? She didn't know which '1' came first', Michaela Shear-Dawson stood up to her full and imposing 5' 11" and in her poshest Scarborough accent, loudly said;

"This is quite appalling and you should be totally ashamed of yourself, both for not researching your audience and for mistakenly believing that this discriminatory drivel is in the least amusing. The colour of my hair is part of my being, my style and my choice. Assigning behaviour or personality traits to someone because of the colour of their hair is childish in the extreme.

It is as insulting and as despicable as you gaining cheap laughs based on gender, ethnicity or occupation. (By this time there was rapturous applause and each sentence was punctuated by cheers from the delegates). My colleagues in the room who share my hair colour are some of the most successful women in the business world.

They also share the traits of courage, tenaciousness, ferocious wit and intellect. These are all qualities that seem sadly lacking from your act and appearance here tonight. We are here to be recognised for our achievements, not marginalised for our appearance. You are a very sad pretender to the role of entertainer".

Mickey sat down to riotous applause and a whoop and a high-fives from me. The ventriloquist was the colour of porridge and clearly shock and awe struck. He muttered, almost sobbed, 'I'm dreadfully sorry it wasn't my inten....'. He couldn't get the words out before Michaela was on her feet again remonstrating 'Not you, you fool, that little fellow sat on your lap!'

FREEDOM from BOSSES FOREVER

For once I was speechless. I checked my phone – still no contact from Ant.

Tony Robinson OBE (with Soculitherz)

Chapter Eight

Small is cool

A man is a success if he gets up in the morning and gets to bed at night and inbetween he does what he wants to do.

Bob Dylan
Quoted in Quotable Quotes for Quoters by Aubrey Malone 2005

I'm now on a train and on my way back to London. What am I wearing? Great question and I'll tell you how you can look as good as me. I thought my white crochet cape by Yves Saint Laurent and skinny jeans from French Connection would be rather wasted travelling through Yorkshire and the Midlands, so I went for a discrete leather look that works every time with men and gets women saying 'I wonder how old she is?'. This outfit is always a winner and the whole lot costs under £600 – a third of the price of my YSL cape.

Here's how you can get the 'Leonora returns to civilisation look'. It starts with your face: skip the fake tan – not that I need it – keep skin as pale as you can and use concealer sparingly. Go with your natural glow. You'll wear a black trilby (from Mango), a short, waist hugging, red leather jacket (mine came from Topshop), a black and white dogtooth scarf, black leather fingerless gloves, white trousers and black ankle boots with press studs (such as Ted Baker). Works every time.

Dear reader, you're probably wondering if leaving Scarborough for what might be the last time in my life is a wrench. Well, what's not to like about cinder toffee ice-cream, but I must admit to feeling I can leave most of the Yorkshire men whom I've met far behind me. Listening to Tommy Tatlow's Scarborough radio show yesterday

FREEDOM from BOSSES FOREVER

confirmed again that these are not really Leonora's people. I recorded and have tried to reproduce (didn't understand some of his phrases) the opening extract from his show so that you can see what I mean. This extract starts with his 'catchphrase':

Opening extract from Tommy Tatlow's 'What's on in Scarborough Music Show – Lite Version':

"Evening all. This is Tommy Tatlow – that's two m's and one l and 'Tommy's one 'ell of a DJ'.

I'm bringing you your weekly 'What's on in Scarborough Music Show Lite'. This lite version is the Tuesday shorter version of the Saturday show where we tek out the music, just leaving all my informative comments, even the cock ups – sorry shouldn't have said that – for you to ponder on, and opefully mek you want to go and see some of the dos and turns that are on during the week. That is, those who haven't already been and gone on Saturday night to Tuesday afternoon.

All clear? Clear as the mud they dredged out of Peasholm Park boating lake, I'll bet. As usual I was broadcasting live on Saturday from my front room overlooking the South Bay, just above the Spa, where the cliff lift is, which I've been telling you for weeks now isn't working due to (loud and slow) 'ne..ce..ss..a..ry maint..u..nunce'. Don't you worry, when it's back up and running you'll be the first to know.

So ere goes with Saturday night's show. I think I started out with a bit of a grumble about the number of e-mails and texts I'd had since the last show.

Before I spin the first disc, I just want to mention that we really welcome your e-mails and texts on what you thought about our show and the events you've gone to in Scarborough, which is Britain's first and finest resort, but not, definitely, utterly not, when you cast aspershuns on our unbiased recommendations of the shows you should go and see.

Tony Robinson OBE (with Soculitherz)

For those of you who don't know, this show is a voluntary, unpaid, 'help in the community service' for all Scarborough residents and holidaymakers. We don't take advertising and if we do get free tickets to any of the shows, with or without additional hospitality, it is only so we can describe to you better what's on offer.

So I ope that'll be the end of it and let's play the first CD, which is by that fellah me lad who does the New Year's Eve telly show and who'll be playing live in Dalby Forest in just a few weeks time now, I think, it's – hang on a sec – Jools Holland.

(Leonora note: no music, of course, as this is the lite version with music edited out – so there's just a short silence)

Well, that was Jools Holland, but he was on the piano and not singing. The singer was Norah Jones – very nice looking young lady – but Norah won't be with Jools when he plays in these parts. I'm sure Jools won't mind me calling him Jools as he's not in Scarborough at the moment.

In fact none of the singers on this CD, apart from Jools himself of course, will be in Dalby Forest, as this is one of them duets CDs called... If you want it... well, I'm sure that HMV in Scarborough centre will have it, and it is they who kindly supply all my CDs for this show.

Now, on to the first of this week's tips about what to see in Scarborough. It's tonight at 7.30 and costs £12 and £8 for concessions (make sure you can prove you're ill..edge.. ible). It's in Peasholm Park and it's where the (smack lips noise) wonderful Scarborough Spa Orchestra do their 3 Tenors night, which is a bit similar to that Pavarotti trio, except of course not with Italians and Spaniards. Although one of our three tenors will have travelled from Wales to sing with the (smack lips noise) wonderful Spa Orchestra.

You can tek your own picnic and drinks, but I have to say that what's on offer inside can't be beaten, especially the 'omemade – well baker's shop made – scowwens. Bottles of wine are a very

FREEDOM from BOSSES FOREVER

reasonable £6.50 and you can get those little bottles for £2. If there's more than just you going, then tek a tip from Tommy and share a big bottle betwixt thee: it's best value.........'

Some think it incredible that Tommy T was nominated for a MOBO as best radio DJ along with Rampage, RobboRanx, Semtex and Shortee Blitz. Tommy is undoubtedly a fine ambassador and enthusiast for Scarborough, but I'm not sure that my association with him and other male Tyke gabblers and ranters, like TR, is good for my image.

I realise that Leonora Soculitherz is becoming a brand and that's probably inevitable because of my media exposure. Having recently and reluctantly appointed TR as my agent for when 'Stripping' comes out, I just hope that my brand value is sustainable. His lack of style may be reflected onto me.

I dread accompanying him to events, like the recent launch of my little 'how to' photo book 'Deliverance from IKEA'

My photo book, which you've probably seen in Waterstones, is about revamping old stuff; such as chairs, shelves and chests of drawers. You buy rubbish versions of them for a song in car boot sales, markets and house clearances and turn them into unique, must have new interior furnishings that are all your own work. You add the varnish, the embroidery, the patchwork and the creativity.

It's not unlike my approach to 35-40 year old hunky men with money, but with hairy backs and legs. Steal the man, but wax the body hair off. Then teach them tantric sex. I only got interested in this because I was fed up with Sting going on about it and my girlfriends asking if I'd ever had a man last longer than six minutes. I guessed from experience that three minutes was probably the most for any of us.

Yet anyone can learn through a bit of pulling and a bit of pushing on the bit between the penis and the scrotum how to get them beyond the magical six minute mark. It's just finding a man to let you do it to them that's the problem. Ant was just not interested, but I recommend it: it amuses me for hours and drives the man insane. It must be the frustration of millions of sperm ready to dive in and have a swim but it's as if their toes are stuck to the diving board. Anyway, with men or furnishings, renovate rather than flat pack every time.

Unfortunately for me, as I was with TR, it was a canapés and champagne book launch in a stately home. This is where we are served by waiters and waitresses circulating with their silver trays laden with posh snack food or bubbly. With TR in their midst this will always provide an impromptu, wet, colourful and noisy side show for the assembled guests. I now stay calm by betting with myself just how many trays will become airborne, as I've observed a domino effect from the flying debris and evading bodies.

Am I digressing? The point is that, unlike you 'strippers for freedom' who are just setting out on the road to self employment and freelancing, I have got to the stage where handling my own business and personal affairs is becoming more than a one woman job. I'm sure Paris Hilton has the same problem. Hence I added TR to my team. Sure, I'm offered work for a fee and I'm quite capable of negotiating my own rate and I have a little grey, dull chap who looks after my accounts and handles my tax.

The more amazingly witty television appearances I make lead to more media engagements, book deals and journalists everywhere. The media, understandably, now want my views on everything from muesli to moisturisers and wristbands to wallpaper. I feel that if I tell everyone in future 'talk to my agent', it will give me more space, order and focus in my life. That is, until I remind myself who I've appointed as my agent.

Anyway, in recent years I've never had to look too hard to find work or income, but I realise that very few professionals and executives reading this masterpiece have my natural assets or celebrity status. Indeed, perhaps I succeeded because I'd never been an executive in a corporate environment. This can actually work against you being able to succeed when working for yourself:

67. Stripping for freedom requires you to depilate yourself of the corporate mumbo jumbo and gobbledygook that gets in the way of selling and doing work.

Nothing proved this more to me than a business woman I encountered on the second part of my train trip, from York to London.

Opposite me amongst the distressed and suffering in 'Quiet' Coach B on National Express service was Jools. I should explain that the B Quiet zone is usually guaranteed to have a drunken party, snoring businessmen and wailing children in it. When I first started travelling GNER's coach B was the smoking carriage. It is hugely missed.

Jools is a maximum gloss, minimum brain business woman. Like my fellow inmates, I didn't know Jools before our journey began, but we all feel we know her well now and sincerely hope we never meet her again.

We know her name because she made four mobile phone calls on the way to London and each time shrieked 'Hi-ya this is Jools – so how are you?' The recipient will, undoubtedly, have been reaching for both valium and ear plugs. However, an hour into the journey the stricken passengers of Coach B would have answered her rhetorical question with: 'Ready to stuff that mobile phone down your throat, or even where the sun never shines – OK Jools?'

Jools failed to respect us with even a minute's silence out of the whole 130 minutes ordeal – 7,800 executive drivel-filled seconds. Her language was not unusual for a corporate executive, but there was just too much of it and it was in no comprehensible order. I hated it and kept a tally. So we had plenty of the usuals such as 'kit', 'blue skying', and 'out of the box' but, more unusually, 8 repeats of 'core sourced', 12 of 'outsourced'. 18 of 'high impact', 23 of 'positive feedback', 28 of 'having a panic on', 42 'cool, cool, definitely,

definitely', 49 'bollocked' and 97 (high pitched with an almost sung, long finish) 'Oh...My...Goooooooooood!'. Ironically, there were also 6 'So in a nutshell that's where we are.'

As I walked to the carriage door to get off the train I noticed a memory stick on the seat behind me, which I picked up. Out of the corner of my eye as I walked down the platform I noticed one of those young, Boss suited guys with the now distinctive comms watch and wicufflinks. 'Tochen', I thought and now they're following me.

Later I realised that he may have not been looking for me, but for the memory stick. No big deal, as there doesn't seem a day when someone doesn't find a government disk or memory stick with sensitive data on it lost on public transport. On mine were Department of Work and Pensions records, Health Service records, Credit records and Local Council records. The memory stick was the property of the Department of Insurgency.

Some of the names were highlighted and I could only assume that these were fat or disabled or smokers, self employed or unemployed people from ethnic minority communities or disadvantaged communities with poor credit histories or mortgage arrears or no pension. I couldn't really tell and sometimes even this supercool fashionista thinks she knows nothing at all. Which comes first, the act of terrorism to justify the government databases or the government databases which need an act of terrorism to justify them?

Within seconds of leaving the train, without signing any autographs, I was sitting outside a bar near Kings Cross, dragging on a Marlborough Light: being this slim isn't all pilates and sipping an Archers and Lemonade.

My first task at precisely 9.48 a.m., was to use my name as a journalist who appears in the best papers, to get the Department of Insurgency to agree to see me. I would then return the memory stick in exchange for a few answers to my questions. Success! Next, I began to scribble down what I'd learned from my near death (Jools's death) experience. Jools is proof positive of the need to 'strip for freedom.'

At least one in five (moving towards one in three) professionals and executives are thinking of escaping the rat race and the treadmill of corporate life by starting their own business. Getting your mind, body and lifestyle right will be just as important as your business idea and plans. You are going to sell your body and mind to succeed as an executive going it alone.

This means ridding yourself of a few bad habits you may have picked up as a career corporate executive. Jools gave us a good example of some of the habits to kick. Without a dramatic change in attitude to 'management', as an entrepreneur Jools has 'failure' stamped across her forehead.

Jools has a big ego – no bad thing in itself – but this leads her to see work primarily as an opportunity to confirm and build her status. Jools is treating work as a social activity, with the main objective to be seen and heard by the people by whom she wants to be seen and heard.

Successful entrepreneurs work long hours, but usually spend them either making money or enjoying family and leisure time. At the beginning it's certainly far more of the former. This 'work hard, play hard' trait is very different from most corporate executives, whose working day usually merges the two:

68. A successful entrepreneur understands how precious time is and uses it to the best business advantage.

This is an essential attitude: far more than the skill of 'time management.' Jools knows the importance of, and has been extensively and expensively trained in 'time management', 'motivation', 'innovation', 'giving feedback', 'team building', 'leadership', and 'strategy' (lots of types). Indeed, she'll talk all day about these, but as an entrepreneur would achieve very little. A stripper only makes money for the time he or she shows him or herself in person ('in the flesh'), which is what people will pay to see. Stripping is regarded as the entertainment industry, not the sex industry.

69. The majority of self employed or micro enterprise owners can think about themselves as being in the entertainment industry and giving the audience what they want to see and hear.

The entrepreneur is interested in what customers will pay for, but Jools is interested in what her ego demands and her employer will pay for.

If Jools was working for herself, we'd wait all day and still not hear or see anything anyone would pay for. Jools achieves very little in business terms, primarily because she does what she thinks looks good for her career, rather than what is good for business. As a career manager, the way for her to make more money is to impress people inside her own organisation.

70. The entrepreneur/owner manager doesn't waste time and usually makes money by making as many deals as possible with people outside their organisation.

So, if you want to get out of the rat race, start getting out of your corporate management habits. You'll need to use your time better. You need to bin the corporate lingo and gobbledygook. Jools wasted two hours of business-building time by bossing her P.A. around, telling her boss how wonderful she is and reminding her network that she's on the ball and doing the biz.

Whilst that is occurring, most of my entrepreneur friends will have made several small attempts to move their business forward by making some money. So, recognise that the things corporate executives love doing are a luxury, a potential drag on productive time for the entrepreneur. Searching for and hiring staff, interviewing, meeting, consulting, presenting, planning and travelling are almost perks of a corporate management position, which the entrepreneur most often sees as eating away at business development time.

Forget many of the things you're good at in your corporate existence and work out how you'll spend your time as an entrepreneur. Start your strip for freedom by kicking out these corporate management habits and language. The only thing that would stand Jools in good stead if she started her own business is that she is a woman. Research has shown that not only do women exude class, 'cool' and intelligence, they are also more successful (proportionally more survive and thrive in their business) than men.

Indeed, it is often said that:

71. The worst mistake a woman entrepreneur can make is to get a male business partner and then take on male staff. Men: who needs them?

Although I've still heard nothing from Ant, I have had a call from Dick Rice, the top executive at Shaini's who can get me the interviews I need with the very highest government officials in return for my publisher giving them safe passage to a secret Canadian location. So Ant had been good to his word and all I had to do was meet a chap called Jack later.

Before I moved on to meet all these government officials, there were a few pieces of information about the Tochen network which I thought might be gleaned from one who knows the inhabitants of the Square Mile better than most. I rang K (Kylie); the same blemish free, body-to-die-for K with whom I went to Malta for my initial research for this book.

Leonora: Hi.... just wanted to check something for my book. Wasn't one of the guys you said always comes back to the club to see you the senior partner at that top global consultancy firm – the one who came up with the concept of 'quantitative easing'?

K: 'Yeah but I've moved on from him. He was having his cake and eating it. After getting them to print more money, he thought he could get everything he asked from anyone without giving a reason why. The apologies came and he was like 'I made a big mistake' and I'm like, 'Yeah, yeah I know, go ahead and say whatever you need to say to make you feel OK and able to sleep at night'.

Leonora: Did he ever mention the word 'Tochen'?

K: 'Yeah, yeah like he'd see someone limp into the Club and say 'ah he's into Tochen, must go and say hello.'

Leonora: 'Did he try and get you into Tochen.'

K: 'Nah he was only ever interested in getting into my knickers. Figuratively speaking, of course, as he rarely saw me with them on. He did once go like 'What do you think about this crap that says the economy wouldn't have crashed if women were running the banks and Government? I went like, 'It's not crap, as women wouldn't play the same high risk games, spend half their time being badly dressed in pointless meetings and getting ridiculous salaries and bonuses for phoney jobs. He went like 'No point in taking you to a Tochen meeting then.'

Leonora: 'That all?'

K: 'And he asked for some information on some of the habits of punters in the club which he said was for a Tochen survey on leisure spending – or might have been pleasure spending – I'm not sure.'

Leonora: 'Nothing about God?'

K: 'Nah. He looked the type though: I was waiting for God'

Leonora: 'OK. Thanks K. Oh, one more thing. Did you work out how all the top Tochen leaders just seem to get richer, despite the companies, institutions, departments and countries they run going bust?

FREEDOM from BOSSES FOREVER

K: 'Sure, that's easy. I suppose making big money is like just low risk gambling of big money at the right time. It's always been that way and they have no intention of it ever changing. It's well over the top what they're doing at the moment though. Timing... taking opportunities that no-one else can see and making the money before it all turns to dust. The whole network thing is about getting to or buying a position as near the top of the network as you can, so that you'll get into any new opportunity fastest with the best position. It's like just taking advantage of what they know is going to happen before anyone else does. It's cool – information is power. That's why I can make big money too, just by keeping quiet about what I know.'
'There are only a limited number of legal ways to get rich quick from what you know. Kiss and tell is the fastest, but it's a hell of a lot dirtier work than I'll do. All you do is dress as sluttishly as possible, reveal as much flesh as you can and be seen in Kabaret on Monday, Funky Buddha on Tuesday, Chinawhite on Wednesday and Movida on Thursday. At the week-end it's anywhere in Kensington. There isn't a single premier league footballer who is faithful to his WAG. They've all got lawyers on speed dial because they sleep around. They offer payoffs and you know they've done it before. So get over it Lee (reader, my head feels as if it is about to explode). Whether it's the Tochen network snaring a deal, or a PA from Essex snaring a premier league footballer, there's big money in being shafted.'

Leonora: 'I knew I wouldn't like it.'

K: 'Don't get arsey Lee.'

Leonora: '*Leonora!*'

K: 'Leonora then... it's just what you learned at school and uni... nothing dramatic... nothing to get paranoid about – just capitalism in action. The non dodgy stuff isn't that different from the dodgy stuff. Take a look at any pyramid selling scheme, ponzi scheme, Iraq regeneration scheme, arms for oil deals, Freddie Mac or Enron type scam and you'll usually hear about the little people who lost out. The founder members with multi millions or billions have always made a lot of money before the thing collapses. One, like Bernard Madoff or a few executives, will take the rap but, hey, they've all made the dosh by then and hundreds in both the public and private sector have been in on a very profitable scam. If a few lose their job or even go to prison, it still hasn't prevented all the top positions remaining stinking rich. You should put that in your book as a tip from me:

72. Go where the big money is going, even if you don't understand why it's going there.

After leaving the bar I get off the tube at Oxford Circus, ready to walk to the IoD and then the Savoy Hotel for my meetings. I know you'll think that I've alighted nowhere near my destinations, but first I must buy some shoes. Secondly, after 7/7 when I was in Russell Square and Southampton Row when it all happened, I walk as much as I can in London.

Chapter Nine

Lost In Translation

He knows nothing and he thinks he knows everything. That points to a political career.

Bernard Shaw
Major Barbara Act 3 (1905)

The shoes I buy are nothing flash, just a pair of dogtooth check court shoes with red leather piping and bow and a killer heel. They're a snip at £75 from Dune, The Plaza, 120 Oxford Street. I needed the shoes badly, because on the train I read an article saying 7.5 million women in Britain owned sixteen or more pairs of shoes. Quelle horreur! Try as I might, I couldn't picture more than fifteen of mine.

After my Oxford Street purchase I walked up Regent Street and past the site of the old Café Royal, where Sherlock Holmes was accosted. Incidentally, Holmes' attackers escaped down Glasshouse Street. I carry on past Piccadilly Circus tube and Lilywhites, (never wear shell/track suits, joggers, white tennis socks, white sweatbands or cricket abdominal protectors), heading for Pall Mall. A shortcut for me here would be to veer left past St Martin in the Fields, stopping for a bowl of soup and to give my respects to the greatest 17th century celebrity, actor, royal squeeze and nutritionist – Nell Gwynne – and then down Duncannon Street.

However I don't go this way, because I always like to pop into the Institute of Directors at 116 Pall Mall, even if I haven't a meeting there. It cheers me up and gives me some recompense for my membership fee. I usually just use the loo at the IoD, then have a quick wander around the Directors' Room and Morning Room to

Tony Robinson OBE (with Soculitherz)

laugh at the suits, ties and the price of a glass of wine or cup of coffee.

This morning I do have a meeting though. My meeting, as arranged by phone at Kings Cross, is with Mike Jackson, the UK Head of Insurgency Prevention. This meant a private room, but you still get the same biscuits; in my living memory, however, these never include any chocolate ones.

As a Canadian, I've struggled from time to time to understand the infrastructure of your Civil Service and the responsibilities of your various senior public servants. Their departments and titles always seem to be changing and whilst the top bods always stay in London, they seem regularly to move their departments all over the country at £60 million a throw.

As you know, I've had huge difficulties understanding when they're talking about supporting small businesses, which they call SMEs, so I knew I'd need help to understand Insurgency Prevention and the collection of databases in its name. Consequently I'd hired an interpreter – Don Cruse – through the kind offices of the IoD, (part of their 'introduce a member, get them to the Annual IoD Conference at the Royal Albert Hall and get an interpreter at half price' deal).

Don Cruse is a former astronaut and Tochen networker who freelances as a translator of 'idiosyncrasies, idioms and idiots'. I was sure that the people I needed to interview would be within his sphere of expertise.

After I handed him the memory stick, which he threw in the bin, Mike Jackson kicked off with; 'Good Day Ms Soculitherz. I understand that you want to understand our vision as protector and protection from what we don't know and what we do know means who we've got and who we've got is not for you to know.'

'What did he say Don?'

FREEDOM from BOSSES FOREVER

'Don't expect many answers.'

'OK Mike, thanks for seeing us. I think I most want to understand what your department does and if it is fair and legal?'

'Others have asked that and I can see your direction of travel, but you'll have to ask yourself what we do when there isn't any low hanging fruit. Then the subject matter cannot be either in the public domain or seen as a matter for right or wrong, within the framework of the law or not. It must remain below the radar. You're making a point that deserves our consideration and, of course, if you can provide me with the evidence then I can take it further'

'What did he say Don?'

'He said nothing.'

'Nothing?'

'Nothing.'

'So what do I say next?'

'Tell him you're used to mangling the testicles of obstinate Civil Servants.'

OK. 'Mike. Do you value your balls?'

'Precisely.'

'Mike, if I have a pair of pliers under the table do you know whose low hanging fruit I'm going to go for first?'

'Mine?'

'Precisely. So shall we start again Mike? You've got CCTV on everyone and help from Google too and there are 4 million people on the police DNA database. You're adding data all the time with ContactPoint child protection, the health service patients' register, a national identity register and over 40 other databases and now you're going to store information on every telephone call, e-mail and internet visit made by everyone in Britain? This at a time when up to 3 million people will be unemployed and the small enterprises that make up 99% of UK businesses are being battered by corporates and institutions and need government help to see out the recession. During all this, you're planning to spend £100 billion on information technology for government databases over the next five years. How do you justify this Mike? Who are the insurgents from whom you're protecting us?'

'Leonora, I'd be deserting my post if I didn't do all I could to prevent another 9/11 or 7/7. Insurgents are terrorists, anarchists, protesters, anyone who disagrees with government policy really'

'What did he say Don?'

'It's all about prevention of terrorism.'

'But that's still like saying nothing.'

'Agreed. Tell him you'll chop his dick into little pieces.'

'Mike, I'm not happy. This emery board (readers note: no scissors in my Louis Vuitton clutchbag) could render your penis as useful as your anti-ageism regulations are to women TV presenters, so I'd advise you to answer these questions. Why is it necessary to breach human rights for prevention of terrorism, which organisations are receiving this information and for what purpose?'

'Prevention of terrorism is and will remain our priority but we welcome your views.'

'What did he say Don?'

'Your time's up.'

'But he hasn't answered any of my questions.'

FREEDOM from BOSSES FOREVER

'Look, there's one where we strip him naked and put a 'meanings in the morning' box over his head, tie wires to his fingertips and genitals and tell him that if he drops his arms from an outstretched position we'll fry his meat and two veg. We say that if he falls off the little box on which he's standing on one leg, then we'll release the snakes, spiders and scorpions too. Oh, and we play him Barry Manilow records throughout. It takes a few minutes to set this all up though – how long have you got?'

I stormed out and heard them singing 'Copacabana' before I slammed the door shut. I swore to myself that I'd stick to my original assignment, complete it within 48 hours and then fly back to the relative safety and sanity of Canada.

I continued across Trafalgar Square, onto the Strand, past Charing Cross Station, and into Savoy Court. Savoy Court is the only place in Britain where you drive on the right, but I'm on foot and narrowly avoid being run over. I enter the Savoy Hotel and I spot my civil service mole, Jack, slumped in a white leather seat to the left of the entrance. He's in a confused and dehydrated state because he doesn't think he can put the cost of a Savoy cup of tea on his subsistence allowance form.

He explained he'd had a bad couple of weeks. He was the special adviser to Ministers on how to maximise their allowances and expenses and he was also the civil servant responsible for recruiting Michelle and Michaela of Fabsolutely2Good plc to mastermind the government's blogging strategy to marginalize the opposition.

I said I couldn't believe that Michelle and Michaela would make a wrong call. He said 'They haven't. It's absolutely brilliant and the PM is actually delighted with me. Basically the blogs were never going to be uploaded. It was part of the plan to leak them to the press, then 'outcry', then a couple of resignations and we achieve everything we wanted. The press publishes our slurs on opposition Ministers' sexual habits and illnesses to a far bigger audience than the blogs would have reached. The public says to themselves 'no smoke without fire' and our mud sticks.

Tony Robinson OBE (with Soculitherz)

It was the expenses and allowances work that's really caused the problem. Basically I got sloppy. I'd had a heavy night at the Civil Service Club with a couple of Peers who were celebrating the arrival of some new equipment for the dungeon and I was rushing the next morning to get all the claims in for the Ministers' second home allowances. I had to use up the allowances, as it was the end of the financial year. Anyway, one small item in claims totalling hundreds of thousands cost me dear. I ordered a job lot of writing tables at £400 each on which Ministers could write their expenses and the press picked it up. Stupid: rule number one is always to make all expenses and allowances claims look different then, if challenged, we can make up individual stories on behalf of the Ministers to justify it. I left them without a table leg to stand on'.

Annoyingly, he seems less interested in me than in the fact that I knew Ant Cracie, clearly one of his heroes.

'Any friend of Ant Cracie is a friend of mine. I reckon the reason that he's the first black guy to get to the top of the corporate and self development speakers' circuit is because he's the smartest, most accessible, most pure, most believable, most god fearing fellah that's ever made it from such humble beginnings. Mind, he's got some influential friends now, but what a guy. I'm always scared stiff in front of camera or with a radio mic in front of me, but what I so admire about Ant is that he's always willing to speak to his public and the media. From TV chat shows to radio interviews he'll always give a view.

Unlike some celebrity, leadership and self development gurus who just promote their latest book, he'll give you his opinion on anything from technology to space travel, mysticism to high finance, war to energy supplies, obesity to binge drinking and even haute couture. Anyone who is paranoid must think he's always talking about them. It's like a constant popularity campaign, but it works. He's just so presentable, accessible and wise.

All very interesting, but just at the moment I'm unsure whether I am still a friend of AC. To the business in hand. Jack knew that I'd

FREEDOM from BOSSES FOREVER

received a call from Dick Rice, Chief Operating Officer of the influential World Commodities' Trade Protection Association (Shaini 's for short). Jack had also received instructions from Dick and was to take me to a secret location in Great Scotland Yard, where I would meet two senior government officials who would tell me everything I wanted to know. After the interview they'd been promised a safe passage overseas.

At last I was about to solve the mystery of why the rich fail and still get rich and where the missing £millions of taxpayers' money had gone that were originally earmarked by government ministers to support start ups and owners of small and home businesses.

I was blindfolded on the short taxi ride from the Savoy, (I paid for the coffee at the Savoy and Jack took the receipt), and Jack briefed me that the two senior government officials that I'd meet were mainly, but not solely, responsible for everything, including the lost millions. I asked Jack whether he'd heard of the Tochen network and if I was about to meet a couple of their senior members.

Jack said: 'Everyone has heard of Tochen, although perhaps under different names', and 'I don't know' are the answers.'

He did volunteer immediately that he thought that a third of the £millions allocated in support for small business owners is lost through due process, supply chain and infrastructure costs.

This is how Jack, in his inimitable, pedantic style explained to me how it works:

"What does Government nearly always do before announcing a new policy to support small business owners? It consults with all and sundry, even if it's already made up its mind what the policy is going to be. Now, what if the major telecommunications companies, computer and software manufacturers, office furnishings and office equipment suppliers, property owners, developers and facilities management service providers all came together and ensured they were at the forefront of the consultation? It would mean that any recommendations arising from the consultation phase would be to the benefit of all these organisations.

Isn't it likely then, that in any new, government funded initiative these 'interested parties' would recommend that a new infrastructure be put in place to ensure propriety and quality in the services provided through the public funding? Consequently, a great deal of money intended for prospective and existing entrepreneurs would then go to these 'interested parties'. That way they ensure there are good facilities, from curtains to computers, for all the civil servants allocated to the new infrastructure.

So, in summary, up to a third of all the money allocated to prospective and existing business owners will be used to fund this new infrastructure.

It is also through these large organisations and medium sized businesses that we reach small businesses. There are 33,000 medium and large businesses in the UK and 4.5 million small businesses. Government can't be expected to implement policy with its money, so it gives both the money and support to the large and medium businesses and they can pass it on to small businesses that supply them.

Then we have to decide how we're going to implement the new policy. Let us say the government policy is to provide prospective entrepreneurs with a free or low cost opportunity to learn how to grow their business. What is the process to bring this about?

Well, the policy is passed to a senior civil servant, who recruits or borrows a team of civil servants from a government agency to implement the policy. These civil servants have been taught the importance of using consultants to help them procure services, attend meetings and write papers. Indeed there are now a number of major consultancy practices that also advise civil servants on how to choose the right consultants for each new initiative. Of course, in addition to the fees for meetings and briefings with consultants, there are also the costs for venue, accommodation, food and drink.

FREEDOM from BOSSES FOREVER

So a lot of the budget goes immediately on infrastructure, supply chain, process and consultancy costs, which is probably the case for any new government policy or initiative. It wouldn't matter whether the intended recipients were prospective entrepreneurs, patients, carers or prisoners, they won't get much of the original budget".

'Thanks Jack."

I was still keen to interview the two senior government officials. When the taxi pulled up I paid the driver (and Jack took the receipt). Still blindfolded, I was guided into a building and up stairs to a room.

The smells and noises seemed familiar and I suspected that I was at the Civil Service Club, which I knew to be a care home for public servants whom Government wanted to distract or keep away from their duties. Still no texts or calls from Ant. In the tradition of all good storytellers, I think I'll keep you in suspense for a while before providing the last piece of the jigsaw.

Tony Robinson OBE (with Soculitherz)

Chapter Ten

The Answer is Blowing in the Wind

Tis very warm weather when one's in bed

Jonathan Swift
Quoted in 'Quotable Quotes for Quoters by Aubrey Malone 2005

It was a very short, blindfolded journey from the Savoy Hotel to Great Scotland Yard. What I heard that evening was more frightening than anything I've heard in all my years as a top journalist and celebrity interviewer. Actually that's not true. I was scared stiff today when I read an irresponsible article in the Metro that said "Regular ejaculations lower a man's risk of prostate cancer... between 13 and 20 times a month there is a 14% lower chance of developing the cancer and if you do it 33 times a month you get to a 33% lower chance"

I know some male friends who will interpret these stats. to mean that 100 ejaculations a month will ensure there is no chance of their getting prostate cancer. This was such a frightening thought that I not only destroyed my copy of the free Metro, but every other one in the container, in the hope that any potential partner of mine will never have seen the offending article and hence will not volunteer himself, or me, for this regime of preventative medicine. I think that the author of the piece should be locked up for sexual incitement and provocation of the whole messy business.

Before I tell you how my UK assignment ended, here are some final tips for escaping the rat race by stripping for freedom. By now I expect you to be enterprise ready, fashionable, life-knowledgeable and primed for success like a cocked trigger.

You're also ready to be naked now. Actually, although I love clothes, I always prefer to be naked because clothes make me feel fatter.

73. If you're ready to go into business for yourself, then you're ready to be exposed.

74. You are exposed because whatever status and profile you had when you were employed is stripped away. Your former colleagues and associates will disappear, as they'll be worried you may fail or, worse, you may ask them to do something to help you.

What will make you confident that you can bare your body and mind and go it alone? The answer is

75. Confidence in your body, mind and business idea. You'll get this confidence from test trading – finding potential customers, online and/or offline, ready to pay for your product or service.

First, your body. Treat it mean. Forget about treadmills, bikes, steppers and rowing machines. Go straight for the weights. Apart from my Marlborough Light habit, laxatives and occasional finger down the throat, I put my sleek figure down to a great diet and joining a proper gym. The kind of gym where they sweat, sniff salts, men scratch balls, women kick ass, curse, yell, groan and the weights smash down on the concrete as they let them go. The kind where you only wear black and open your Lucozade Sport drink when no-one's looking in case it takes you more than one go to flip the top.

Then there's the diet. As you're doing weights you don't do Atkins, calorie restrictions or GI indexing – you go straight for the food combining. I recommend the Soculitherz patented, Celebrity Choco-Wine Diet. It means eating chocolate (chocolate sprinkles on cappuccino and ice cream are also allowed) and red wine. Whenever you feel hungry drink more red wine and whenever you feel drunk, eat some chocolate. Your body knows best. Countless research studies have shown that chocolate, red wine and McCain's Oven

Ready chips (must be that Scarborough influence on me) are best for your health, but I go for the latter only as a Sunday morning treat.

What should also give you confidence are the twin assets of your mind and your business idea.

Think of yourself as a guru – the top person in the world with your business idea. What is a guru like? Well they're paid the big bucks for stating the obvious, which equates to them knowing more on a specialist subject than anyone else. Who do they advise? They advise management teams and directors in big companies who often can't see, or aren't motivated to see, the wood for the trees.

They're lost in a parallel world of applying management techniques, jargon, planning, meeting, presenting and handling internal politics:

76. Be encouraged: the guru is usually a small business owner or freelancer telling massive corporations of highly qualified managers what to do.

So how does that work then? One of the reasons for the continuing global meltdown of big companies and major institutions is because their directors and managers are just not as entrepreneurial as small business owners; they're rule and precedent bound, rather than breaking new ground. They wait for marketing to work rather than go out selling. They have to fiddle the books or go for dodgy investments in order to survive, as they can't grow by providing stuff that people want and will pay for. In truth, the more senior they are the less they can do. If they want anything doing they hire a consultant. Often their internal culture has led to them not understanding the real world anymore, so they cannot have the same bias for useful action as someone starting or running their own enterprise.

How can one person businesses like me (and like you're going to be), beat the big companies in the same marketplace?

77. By being quicker, more flexible and more focused. The area where this counts the most is with customers.

Whilst the big companies are planning to do something different, the small business owner can do it. If it goes wrong then no-one will get demoted and it will be done better next time. So throw away the corporate executive kit bag and do the following:

78. Ensure that whenever you get a new idea you research it quickly, (hours and days not weeks and months), minimise the risks and then do it. You can then improve on it after you've done it. Don't be afraid to copy ideas and give them a slight twist.

79. Ensure that at the end of every day you can say you've spent at least 55% of your time on trying to win new customers and/or keep existing customers.

If you're still saying: 'But Leonora, I'm still not sure what my business idea is', then my answer is 'you wimp!', just:

80. Go to the back of this e-book where I've given you all the best free websites for you to use to find business ideas and get great start up help but:

81. Don't use an adviser or investor-director who has no personal experience of starting and running their own enterprise (you've no time for theory).

82. Don't put 'all your eggs in one basket'. Remember that in the current offline and online trading environment there is absolutely no reason why you should only have one income stream or business. You can have products, services and customers in different sectors. You can have your own enterprise alongside distributorships and franchises. You can even be employed and self employed at the same time.

83. Plan for the product/service make-up of your new enterprise, all income streams and resultant cashflow in the same way as you would plan the preparation of your positions for face-to-face deal making: you need an ideal, a realistic and a fall back.'

Before you ask me any more questions that make me angry, I want to end my book and UK assignment by describing to you what I found in that darkened room of the Civil Service Club. It was more surprising than any of my previous surprises there – and there have been an eerie few. I've had a leaking shower from an empty room above, ghostlike screams from the small bore loo and found a half eaten chicken pie and empty screw top, quarter bottle of Chardonnay in the top drawer of the dresser, next to the Gideon's Bible.

Jack knocked on the door of a first floor room. The door was opened by a tall, young American in a black suit with the now familiar Tochen accessory of a black faced watch with silver numerals and black leather strap. He took me inside, leaving Jack outside, and then removed my blindfold. He pointed to the two senior government officials at the far end of the room, whispering:

'You can have fifteen minutes with these two former leading government officials. One is American and one is British. You may suspect that you know them, but if you ever try to reveal their names we will immediately prove you to be a liar. Right now one of them is speaking at a major charity conference in New York and the other is playing tennis with Cliff Richard and later tonight will be staying with Robin Gibb at his holiday home. Both will have been photographed by the world's media at this time today'.

I didn't feel it was appropriate to ask who Cliff Richard was but I am wary of people with a forename for a surname.

I never saw their faces as they were wearing 'Meanings in the Mornings' boxes on their heads, but I learned a lot about them from their voices and hands. The hands especially: one was probably mid to late fifties and the other one, with the American accent, was probably late fifties to mid sixties.

The younger one I nicknamed the 'Evangelist' because of his insistent but reasonable, yet annoyingly preaching and paternalistic tone. The little pads of skin on his fingertips were a giveaway that he spent much of his time playing the guitar. The more butch one, whom I nicknamed the 'Cowboy', had the hands of someone who didn't spend much time working or indoors, probably interested in country sports – hunting and shooting, that kind of thing.

They were clearly in love as their hands touched regularly. The Cowboy kept reminding the Evangelist throughout that I hadn't come there to hear the Evangelist speak. They weren't immediately aware of my presence. As I sat down, I realised they were debating what the criteria might be for England to be admitted as the '51st state of the USA'. I coughed, (I'd thrown the boiled sweet in the bin but swallowed the paper wrapper), and then I introduced myself.

I wasn't nervous, in fact I felt rather proud of myself that I, a Canadian, a celebrity writer/ journalist, a television presenter and a fashion icon, was doing what the entrapment teams at the Sunday tabloids had failed to do. Namely, to solve the mystery of why the big chiefs continue to get rich when they've totally failed and made us poor plus, of course, where the missing £millions of taxpayers' money are that were supposedly earmarked to support small and home business owners in England.

Naturally, despite my awesome interrogation technique, the 'Cowboy' and 'Evangelist' weren't that bothered about spilling the beans, as I was just a minor delay – irritant perhaps – before they were given safe passage to their secret new love nest in the Pukaskwa National Park in Ontario.

I won't report everything the two cereal boxed lovers said, as reported speech can be a bit tiresome. I have a friend, Lizzie, who does the 'he goes', then 'she goes' then 'I go' stuff for ages when trying to make a point and invariably forgets what point she was going to make.

In my precious fifteen minutes I didn't really learn much about them as individuals. My icebreaker was to ask what made them choose a cave in Canada? The Cowboy said that all the luxury caves on the Pakistan/Afghanistan border were taken, which I knew to be the case from Mickey, whose new 'Escape2Your Dream Cave' timeshare business was booming. I also asked the 'Cowboy' if he'd ever been to New Bedford or Nantucket Island and he said he had.

I'd spotted his gold cufflinks which came from the shops in that particular area. Nantucket and New Bedford are about 850 kilometres due east of Toronto. This is where the centre of the thriving American whaling industry was, right up until the discovery of petroleum in 1859, after which the US whaling fleet was decimated from its high of 700 vessels. I became interested in researching whaling after visiting Whitby, near Scarborough. I found out that whaling, like waterboarding, was a fairly addictive pursuit and that internationally, members of both fraternities weren't afraid to show off about their sporting passions.

Of course America subsequently did as well in farming the new oil as it did in farming whales. What it couldn't get from exploration, it could get by acquisition. Anyway, the sperm whale symbol on the cufflinks of the 'Cowboy' was a giveaway. I was just dying to ask him if he'd done that 'squeeze, squeeze, squeeze all the morning long' jerk circle, kneading of the sperm stuff that they do in Moby Dick but I wasn't quite sure how to phrase my question and I was very short of time.

I quickly realised that these were two deeply religious men and on numerous occasions they referred to their work being a mission from God and that God was their judge. I got the impression therefore, that criticism from me or others about what they'd done and not done to help the economy or small business owners was regarded by them as meaningless. A telling statement, I thought, came early on in

FREEDOM from BOSSES FOREVER

our interview when the Evangelist said 'All great leaders do God, it's as important as being clean shaven and not wearing brown suits'.

So, they made it clear that what they did was their business and they answered to God alone. They promised that I'd also understand why any criticism of their enterprise policies was unjust, when they explained the concept of natural enterprise and how regions must self determine, within the framework they've provided, the support natural enterprise should get and the sanctions unnatural enterprise must suffer.

From time to time I could sense some tension between them. This usually occurred when the Evangelist became reticent about answering certain of my questions. Then he would usually respond 'I'd prefer not to ', to which the Cowboy would interject either 'but you will!' or 'now Chuckles, there'll be no more rides in my aeroplane for you if you carry on like that'.

Every now and again they'd also break off to whisper to each other, presumably to agree what they could and couldn't say and I thought I heard the Cowboy whisper that he'd have to 'loop back with Rum and Condo' but whether 'Rum and Condo' was a professional firm of advisers or a cocktail, I wouldn't know.

I asked whether they thought they'd find it hard living in a cave? They said no-one would ever find them, but they would still be very active, and could even appear in and manage the media whenever they needed to. They said I wasn't to think of their cave as a cold, stark place, because it was a warm, luxurious nest from which they could pursue their hobbies undisturbed. At the prices Mickey charges for dream caves I'd certainly expect them to be very comfortable, with all mod cons.

I've reproduced below what I feel was the interchange that went to the very heart of the matter.

I said: 'I want to find out the answers to two questions. Firstly, why don't the one in seven of the adult workforce in England who are starting or running their own enterprises get their fair share of regulatory assistance, incentives, finance and publicly funded support and training to help them to start up, survive and thrive? Secondly, despite the public outrage in both your countries, why do you allow those who have failed the economy and society to continue to get rich?'

They both answered as one, almost as if they'd been programmed to say it: "It saves time and we always fulfil our promises".

I explained what I'd found out already. That Government states that '£billions are being committed to SME support', but in reality fewer than 5% of UK enterprises (including the 4.5 million small and home office business owners and the 400,000+ start ups each year) actually see any of it. All they see are vast amounts of money being spent on big Corporates, civil service salaries, consultants, infrastructures, processes and marketing to tell us how good the infrastructures and processes are.

I followed this up by explaining that I knew that many millions of the pounds originally intended for prospective or existing small business owners went into funding the building I suspected we were in. I said that it was really an expensive Care Home with varied subsidised trips and activities, a good dungeon, fine food, alcoholic drink and recreational drugs for the residents. I told them I knew that the residents were troublesome peers and civil servants whom Ministers wanted to sideline. 'It's a fair cop guv' said the Evangelist and the Cowboy said 'We plead guilty to both counts'. They giggled.

The Evangelist then explained their joint vision for what types of enterprise were acceptable or 'natural' and what were not.'

'It's about pushing the needle. Basically, we sideline public servants who might support 'unnatural' enterprise. This is in the public interest. We have to ensure that all the government support goes to natural enterprise, but of course we will support offenders who may have been involved in petty crime such as fraud, gambling or

FREEDOM from BOSSES FOREVER

misleading investors plus, by exception, other enterprising individuals not currently in mainstream economic activity.'

I then asked 'Why does nearly all the government money go to the 'usual suspects' i.e. the 100,000 bigger organisations – despite the fact that employment opportunities are reducing in these organisations, when at present most people have the stark choice of either unemployment or self employment? Why is there no interest in giving people the skills and know how to start their own enterprise? Isn't it true that enterprise, despite being the fastest growing sector and career, is always ignored by policymakers?

The Cowboy said 'once we've explained to you 'natural enterprise' most of your questions will be answered. I gave in and nodded 'OK'.

'We leave bottom fishing to the trading floor. Natural enterprise starts at the top of the supply chain with proper leaders and managers, and that's where we get the growth from,' started the Evangelist. 'Large corporations that control the world's natural resources and wealth understand most about natural enterprise. It's a just-add water way of looking under the bonnet. You know as well as I do that big is beautiful, the best things come in big packages, go big on futures, go large on number 17 at roulette and size matters. To put it another way – swallow the frog, shoot the puppy and don't screw the pooch. Proper leaders in big Corporates and institutions know both ways on the strategic staircase and 110% know it is their social and economic duty to ensure that any little business people follow their lead. We prefer to change the régime if they don't understand this.'

The Cowboy added 'You must realise that this mission for natural enterprise is not just a US aspiration, but that a global harmonisation and transformation process is in progress. It's been damned complicated and it's meant going to bed past my bedtime. Sometimes we've felt we've been feeding and riding every horse in the race, and certainly without Condy, Wolfy, Chainy, Rumsy and the Projecty for a Newy Americany Century I don't think we'd ever have been able to find or fix all the facts to our policies – but we did. We did prevail, we will oil prevail and mission accomplished. Onwards and upwards. We all need to blow off steam sometimes.'

The Evangelist then explained that this was why 'government Ministers in the UK were told never to refer to increasing support for 'small business owners', but always to refer to them as 'SMEs' as this refers to 99% of all UK enterprises and gives far more opportunity only to feed the proper, bigger businesses, rather than the little tiddlers. Only fuss with the big stuff. It's the little stuff in life and work that always takes up too much time, particularly hunting for it, for example, weapons. At my house we're always losing little Wii accessories – weapons and racquets – and just yesterday my son lost my favourite Jimi Hendrix plectrum'.

Seizing my opportunity to get in the edgeways word I said: 'I can tell you how to use tights to deal with that problem.' (Dear reader, at this end point in the book, I would welcome some spontaneous applause for how I've used your English words throughout. Remember, to us Canadians, pants are trousers, tights are leggings and pantyhose are tights).

I explained how I used tights to help me find all those little things like lost buttons and butterfly fasteners behind earrings. 'Simply cut off one of the legs, slip it over the nozzle of your hoover (keep it in place with an elastic band) and point it where you think you dropped the little bugger. As long as you didn't have any holes in the foot of your tights then the lost article will be sucked up but will not go up the nozzle. Voila! One Jimi Hendrix plectrum returned to its proud owner.'

The Evangelist seemed to ignore my handy tip and appeared a little narky with me. He hissed, 'The heads up is this. You can't turn a tanker around with a speed boat. What state would the world be in if we didn't train hundreds of civil servants to use diagnostics to filter out the 'disposables'? This is how we net the elephant in the room – we have to pick winners as there's not enough bandwidth. Finding the right corporate leaders for the future is an expensive process.

FREEDOM from BOSSES FOREVER

The headhunters require big fees and the leaders require big salaries, bonuses, pensions and extras on the side.

Even the junior gofers – for example the average local council chief executive with £180,000 salary – will retire with an annual pension of over £100,000. It's not cheap to find these people and look after them until they want to retire, you know. It's a big ask, but we have to knife and fork it. Little enterprises led by unprofessional, sometimes uneducated business owners often have few, if any, such leaders or staff and must be regarded by Governments the world over as disposable. It's OK if they survive, but it's just churn if they don't. My door isn't open on this issue'.

The Cowboy added 'Water is a good test. I like to see whether they sink or swim, especially with weights on and a cloth over their mouth. If they swim but still disagree with us, then frankly it is so unnatural that our respective regulatory and tax authorities will destroy them. Sometimes they swim to their sell by date and if they are high public profile, we ask them to then move aside and we give them a safe haven. We then pay terminally ill look-alikes to play out the end game. We deal with those who want to keep swimming regardless by telling everyone that they are clearly past their sell by date', 'increasingly an embarrassment' or 'no longer relevant', or we just fatally damage their reputation. One way or another we always ensure that the cream remains at the top. It may seem like tokenism, but those who play our game to our rules and in our network are always going to be very well rewarded, even in retirement.'

I didn't understand. It all seemed mad. I was beginning to get as flustered as when the Scarborough seagulls drop their bombs on my Gucci mules. Flashing before me were the words of Sir Michael Graysting when he said: 'Political leaders at the very top may have been to the right universities, but they are only asked to be presenters of prescribed policies. They may not be the sharpest knives in the drawer'.

I wasn't totally certain they were still talking about small business owners. Nevertheless, I had found out where the missing £millions had gone – these two have given it all to their mates.

So we're nearly done. If you want to learn more about stripping for freedom or solving the mysteries of the government's millions feeding the already rich, instead of helping prospective and existing small and home business owners, then talk to my new agent, TR.

I've saved what I think is the best Leonorism to the end. It came from Michel, that rather strange ex French Legionnaire but successful entrepreneur – a French word I believe. It is called *'Working trois pots to make your little pot of money'*.

Translated into English, Michel says:

84. 'Every day when you're running your own enterprise you have to top up pot un, which has in it the details of prospective customers you've yet to contact.

85. Every day you must also contact those in pot deux, which is the pot of prospective customers with whom you're now actively in contact and influencing to buy from you.

86. Finally, every day, you have to contact customers in pot trois who are buying from you, in order to keep them happy and see if they have any referrals that you could put into your other two prospective customers' pots.

87. Do this every day with your offer(s) which all trois pots want and can afford and you will be an entrepreneur par excellence'.

I'm now on a flight back to Toronto and guess who I'm sitting next to in first class? Sir Richard Branson – no, just kidding. It's now over two weeks since I last heard from Ant; I don't expect to hear from him again. His last text to me said:

FREEDOM from BOSSES FOREVER

'Leonora, I'll never forget you.'

-------Finis -------

Tony Robinson OBE (with Soculitherz)

Postscript

Soculitherz has not written any more books on enterprise but she has continued to blog on the subject. You can follow her blogs on the Google No 1 ranked, The Small Business Blog http://sme-blog.com

Here is an example of her work which links to the e-book you have just read:

3 useful questions to ask your start up adviser:

Django Unchained

OMG! What a week it's been. World Book Week and International Women's Day and what the heck is the use of having the inept Tony Robinson OBE as your agent? I will have to let his children and wife have their way and just drive him to a care home – I've run out of excuses for him. He was asked to put forward his 'must read' book for business or when travelling. Instead of my best seller – 'Stripping for Freedom' – he says 'Wuthering Heights'. Instead of putting me forward for International Woman of the Year- supreme fashionista, fearless investigative journalist, a Canadian and Jimmy Choo's hottest model – he says 'Kate Bush'!

Frankly, a care home is too good for Robinson, he'll just sit in a chair watching sport on telly and eating cinder toffee ice cream all day. There is a scene in 'Django Unchained' that I could try out with him in my dungeon – a kind of final warning. Anyway talking of being in a vulnerable position, I've said before that, wherever you are in the world, getting the right help to prepare and start your own business isn't easy. Yet it's just so important. Four out of five start-ups survive longer than three years if they get the right help but as few as two out of five survive that get no help or the wrong help.

Snake Oil Salesmen

Once you've started you can plug into the wonderful Enterprise Rockers Movement and be helped by fellow micro business owners but who do you get to help you when you're preparing to start up? It's not helped by the business opportunity industry, including government schemes, all saying that if you start up with them you'll be fine. Snake oil salesmen the lot of them. Often they just want to sell you something – 'a loan', 'a bank', 'insurance', 'a pension (wtf!)' 'a franchise', 'a mlm scheme' 'a membership scheme', a comms package', a tech package', 'a mentor', 'a coach', 'an adviser', 'self employment rather than employment or unemployment' and so forth. You won't get a woman trying to con you like these guys. Who knew?

It doesn't matter whether you pay for help or get the help free, from a government scheme or charity, but you must get the right help. Someone with more business experience than you is just not good enough. You might get an ex bank manager for goodness sake – thanks but no thanks. Checking qualifications won't help you choose the right person either. My hapless and hopeless agent has mentor, coach, trainer and post-graduate HR and Marketing qualifications but he admits all his qualifications and business experience were of no use to him in starting any of his, totally rubbish, businesses.

The Three Questions

So what I've done to help all potential start-ups, in exchange for them recommending Stripping for Freedom' as the must read book of the century, is give you three questions to ask an adviser, coach or mentor before you decide whether to work with them or not. Naturally, there'll be other questions you want to ask to check if there's a match, but always include these three:

1. Tell me about your business and others that you've helped start up and how they relate to the business I'm looking to start?

2. What do you know about helping start ups to bootstrap rather than borrow?

Tony Robinson OBE (with Soculitherz)

3. How will you help me to test trade so that I know that I can gain customers for my products/services?

Next time, I'll tell you about how to fire your agent.

By the way I, Tony Robinson OBE, also write blogs for The Small Business Blog http://sme-blog.com

FREEDOM from BOSSES FOREVER

Useful websites

Here are my favourite places in the cloud which will give ideas, opportunities and advice in order to free yourself from bosses forever by 'going it alone' in your own business. These are UK sites unless stated.

http://sme-blog.com (Global)
This site is fantastic with everything you need and regular blogs from twenty or more of the best experts on thinking of, starting up and running your own enterprise. It also links to http://WinWeb.com which has an app or cloud software for everything you may require to market (including social media) and operate your business – 'cheap as chips'.

http://EnterpriseRockers.co.uk and http://EnterpriseRockers.com
This is the alternative to reading, where you can find real, live business owners around the world trading together, bartering and supporting each other in one wonderful community. You can join in free and ask questions on Facebook and LinkedIn too.

http://succeedasyourownboss.com (U.S/Global)
The Small Biz Lady, Melinda Emerson, is one of the most influential entrepreneurs in the world and talks terrific sense about starting and running your own enterprise. This is a massive site which will give you great ideas and a lot of low cost and free ways to make a successful start-up. There are excellent videos too.

http://www.enterprisequest.com
For practical help every week there is nothing better than signing up, free, to get the Enterquest bulletin. It has lots of fabulous business ideas, tips and gives low cost and free ways of winning customers, managing cashflow and getting off to a profitable start.

http://www.startupdonut.co.uk/
There are many donuts, such as Marketing Donut, but the one you

Tony Robinson OBE (with Soculitherz)

need at the beginning is this one – Start Up Donut. Can't praise it too highly – a massive, wonderful resource.

http://www.startups.co.uk/
This is packed with advice, ideas/opportunities and help. A fantastic starting your business resource.

http://sybmagazine.com
more of everything you need – biz opportunities/ideas/franchises/guidance/videos/interviews etc

http://bizoppsuk.com
more business opportunities

http://business-opportunity-review.co.uk
yet more business opportunities

http://startinbusinessguides.co.uk
this puts together hundreds of guides for different types of business. Ever thought of being a private investigator or opening a café – it's all here.

http://freelancer.com (Global)
We've included this for two reasons. Firstly, it is important to see how you can earn money from freelancing and secondly, this is a way you can get work done for you in your new business at the lowest cost, with proven reliability. The best site in the world for being a freelancer and using freelancers, in our opinion.

www.enterprisenation.com
free resources and yet more useful videos to help you start your business from home, but also to trade globally from home

www.homebusiness.org.uk
working from home & home business opportunities – great newsletter/club

FREEDOM from BOSSES FOREVER

www.mybusiness.co.uk
resources and guidance for small businesses

www.bcentral.co.uk
Microsoft's small business advice site – lots here

www.everywoman.co.uk
resources for women entrepreneurs

www.smallbusinessadvice.org.uk
links and articles on starting/running a biz

www.ukbusinessforums.co.uk
lively and v. helpful business forums

www.primeinitiative.org.uk
helps people over 50 to go it alone

www.readytostart.org.uk
helps people with disabilities to start up from the wonderful Leonard Cheshire charity.

Tony Robinson OBE (with Soculitherz)

ABOUT THE AUTHORS of Freedom from Bosses Forever

Soculitherz is a Canadian fashionista, investigative journalist and author of this, 'the funniest book on enterprise'. Soculitherz is also a Global Ambassador for the Enterprise Rockers Community. This is free to join, once you have started your business, and makes life better for micro-enterprises everywhere. See http;//EnterpriseRockers.co.uk and http;//EnterpriseRockers.com

Leonora Soculitherz was born in Ottawa and graduated in English and Canadian Literature from Toronto University. In 1990 she married the famous English cellist and composer Gerard Brown and settled in London. Her first book, published in 1991, was a manual for self discovery and fulfilment called 'Enhancing Life in Lemon or Peach'. This had sufficient success for Leonora to begin weekly columns on fashion, self fulfilment and nutrition in a number of journals and magazines.

Separated from Gerard Brown, after a well publicised and televised incident during Elgar's Cello Concerto in 1992, Leonora moved to Corfu. It was in Corfu that she wrote her best selling and Kanawa International Book prize winning first novel, 'The Edible Desire'. This was hailed as a classic of 'magical realism' and was quickly followed up by 'Bong in the Orange Grove', which was made into the film 'Sweet Oranges, Bitter Lemons'.

In the early noughties, seeming to tire of the book and film promotion circuit, Leonora was heard more on radio, back in England once again. She hosted her own popular, weekly Country and Cajun Music show and also did special interviews of famous personalities from the worlds of show business, politics, sports and business, particularly on the causes of their 'inner drive'. She continued to write for the quality press and published her autobiography 'Over Strung and Under Nourished' at the end of 2002.

FREEDOM from BOSSES FOREVER

In 2004 the mythical Soculitherz worked for the first time with Tony Robinson OBE to write her first book on best business practice entitled 'Buzzing with the Entrepreneurs'. She called the experience 'unforgettable' and has been seen infrequently in the UK since. In 2009, enticed by a large advance, she agreed to collaborate with Robinson, for a maximum of forty days. The result was 'Stripping for Freedom'. 'Stripping' was updated and improved by Tony Robinson OBE, in 2013/14, to become 'Freedom from Bosses Forever' much to the disgust of Soculitherz.

Tony Robinson OBE co-founded, the free-to-join-in, Enterprise Rockers Community Interest company, with the fabulous Tina Boden, in January 2012. Enterprise Rockers is a global self help community making business life better for micro (0-9 employees) business owners. Tony writes and speaks on enterprise and is one third of the '#MicroBizMatters Show' which helps employees of large companies and the public sector provide higher levels of customer service to business owners.

Tony Robinson OBE (with Soculitherz)

You can follow Tony at http://TonyRobinsonOBE.com and http://EnterpriseRockers.co.uk

On Twitter he is @TonyRobinsonOBE and @EnterpriseRocks

He is also on LinkedIn, Facebook, Google+, Pinterest and YouTube as Tony Robinson OBE

Since 1986 his other enterprise, which he founded with his best friend, Clare Francis, BAB the Business Advisory Bureau Limited, allows him to guide and coach individuals who want to go it alone as independent professionals. Many are executives facing redundancy or just desperate to cut the chains of the corporate cubicle. They, or their employer, choose to pay BAB as a high quality, private sector alternative to government funded start up support.

Tony is regarded by his peers as one of the UK's leading experts on enterprise - promotion, engagement, policy, skills and development. He was honoured to receive from Prince Charles at Buckingham Palace, in 2001, an OBE for services to small firms and training. In 2012 he received from the IAB, at the House of Commons, a Lifetime Achievement Award for Enterprise. In December 2013, Start Your Business Magazine, gave him a Lifetime Achievement Award for his contribution to enterprise support.

He tries to bring humour into all his speaking engagements and writing on the micro enterprise revolution throughout the world and has researched the essential skills to succeed in your own enterprise. He has spoken at over 140 enterprise and entrepreneurship conferences in the UK and overseas. He is the author of seven books of which this is his 'pride and joy'. He writes blogs and articles on enterprise for many global publications including http://sme-blog.com and http://businesszone.co.uk

A Final Piece of Fun?

Here's a Glossary of Terms used in the corporate world that this e-book will help you to escape from. Where Soculitherz is unsure of the true meaning of the gobbledygook – she has guessed.

A

Actioning: Possibly about doing something.

Added Value: And one for the pot.

Additionality: Displacement.

A ground floor opportunity: It'll never get off the ground.

A loss leader: Hopefully everyone will forget it about it in a few weeks' time.

Anchorade: Releasing bubbles of creativity and energy from right side of the brain by shaking hands with oneself. (A Soculitherz original word).

A need to be proactive: We might as well get drunk.

Approximeeting: Meet at a rough time, details to be sorted out by mobile.

A raft of initiatives: A whole range of equally useless ideas.

A total quality approach: Consultancy income generation plan.

At the end of the day: I don't understand a word I've said, but.../ I can't even be bothered with what I'm about to say.

Auspiced by: Ordered by.

Awareness Building: A promotion that didn't work.

B

BAB, The Business Advisory Bureau Limited: All donations gratefully received.

Belly up: When the raft sinks because the plank develops woodworm.

Big Ask: Impossible.

Bluejacking: Sending an anonymous message from one Bluetooth-enabled handset to another.

Blue-sky thinking: Cloud free, bright ideas that'll never fly.

Boiler Room: Pumping and dumping by brokers

Bottom Fishing: Rude, crude and desperate angle by traders wanting to hook bargain shares after pushing out the boat.

Brain detox: 24 hours of upside down sleep with essential oils' Head massage.

C

Check we're singing off the same hymn sheet: Your alibi is best

Close of Play: er... 5.30/6/6.30/7.00 after 50/90 overs – what?

Coalition of the Willing: Not the greatest alliance in history.

Colleagues: Adversaries.

Colour Your Language: Influencing technique by using predominant colour of client's clothing in speech e.g. 'Have you read (red) my report?'

Conversate: Talking crap.

Cultural considerations: Reasons for saying No!

D

Desk-Yeti: Similar to a desk monkey (someone who spends all day working) but rarer. So rare, in fact, they have never been seen.

Dodgy dossier: The name for the government report into Iraqi weapons which used a student's thesis and our progress reports to the bank manager that have numbers in it. In fact any report from us with numbers in it.

Drill down: Look at.

Drill Up: Going above the original idea/ positive upwards view of the world (devotees seen wearing sunglasses on top of head).

E

Elephant in the room: Big and obvious. Elephants are afraid of mice which is why you rarely see elephants in the board room.

Embed: Shorthand for a journalist living and travelling with coalition forces, for turning in early, or another obscure civil service term used at meetings with business people who wished they'd stayed in bed.

Emotoe Intelligence: Toe to brain positivity by keeping toes wiggling e.g. chocolate or croissant. (Original phrase coined by Soculitherz)

Eradihair Destressing: by daily hunt for (and eradicating) stray body hair. (Original phrase)

Evaluation: Can somebody tell me what we've done and why we did it?

Exit Strategy: Phrase falling into disuse as only now affordable by bankers, politicians and civil servants.

F

Feed through the pipeline: Sell or supply.

Flag Up: An eye watering point.

Flash mob: Brief fad in the summer for spontaneous text organised groups to turn up somewhere, seemingly at random and do a bizarre thing. Also for TR to turn up, unsure of what he's meant to be doing, 200 miles away from where he should have been.

Freedom fries: US re-brand of French fries.

G

Get all my ducks in a row: Excuses in the right order.

Get into bed with: A jump into the unknown with a sleeping partner.

Gideons: Tochen term for people who misplace memory sticks with sensitive government data but are never seen doing it.

Go Forward Together: Linking arms and skipping into the sunset.

Governator: Term used for the former governor of California and Scarborough council leaders.

Granularity: A bit of a show stopper.

H

Heads Up: Recommended in sea or sky but not when looking under the bonnet.

High Altitude View or Helicoptering: What you get from heads in the clouds.

Hot Desking: One step before the departure lounge.

Human Resource Development: Body building – usually bottom up.

I

Idea Showers: Usually done in a lighter hat than brainstorming.

J

Juggling too many balls: Probably a man thing.

Jump the Shark: Out of the jaws... silly solutions to sell the same, sad stuff.

Just-add-water: High cost fat cat leadership development prog. – involves making cup-a-soup.

K

Kippers: Kids in parents' pockets exhausting retirement savings (Three of them lodge in TR's house in Scarborough – any ideas gratefully accepted).

Knife and fork it: Follow up problem solving course after the Just-add-water, fat cat leadership devpt prog – mugs and bibs not allowed in board room.

L

Leading Edge: Meaningless phrase to be used in a mission statement.

Living the values: Hanging on to my job for dear life.

Loop Back: Capturing your colleagues before they cascade down.

M

Macro Management: Big, fat, lazy cat who can't be bothered to find out what his staff does (gambles all the reserves on a rigged roulette wheel).

Managing change: We might have to do something different tomorrow.

Marmite: Closing technique by making yourself either really loved (want to buy now to get into bed with that salesperson) or really hated (want to buy now to get away from that salesperson). (A Soculitherz original)

Matrix management: Jack and Jill in a box.

Mission Statement: Why are we in bed together anyway?

N

Nano: PDQ or when you get chance.

Navel Gazing: All fluff and nonsense.

Net, net: The real bottom line, probably also useful for bottom fishing.

Networking: A group of adversaries bonded by a common desperation.

O

Occupational Qualifications: A sea of apathy for floating numerous & standards methodology rafts.

Outwith: Not in.

P

Paradigm Shift: That'll be the 10 'til 6, music facing, cake eaters and plate steppers.

Poliscam: Tochen method to boost income by factor of five yet give no added value. Used by many politicians with expense allowances.

Positive Outcomes: Better than a poke in the eye from a sharp stick – who knows?

Pre-plan: Er... no such thing.

Prime mover: A sitting target.

Push the needle: The needle in question is on a speedometer. Similar to pushing the envelope but so fast it burns out to nothing.

FREEDOM from BOSSES FOREVER

R

Radar: As in 'beneath', or 'appearing on' – usually means they think you and your idea are going nowhere.

Rapid Smiling: Influencing technique through 5 smiles per 20 seconds (devotees can be seen practising in mirrors, shop windows and shiny shoes). (A Soculitherz original)

Rationalisation: Amputation of bits that are easiest to remove.

Ratio Analysis: An Admiral related to Nelson and useful with sea changes and rafts of initiatives.

Reality Check: Actually it will only need a toilet break to consider, be underwhelmed by and reject your daft proposal.

S

Screw the pooch: As in we haven't got time for you to sit around doing more obscene things to our economy.

Sexed Up: Making something more compelling or interesting than it really is – term originates from Westminster.

Sea change: Let's jump into the lifeboats.

Serious Players: Others more influential than you lot.

Shoot the puppy: Only for alpha males who need to act more deplorably than grasping nettles, swallowing frogs or biting bullets.

Sitcom: Single income, two children, oppressive mortgage – but I think you should donate funds to the kippers (see above and e-mail tony@entrepreneursuk.com).

Ski-ing: Spending the kids' inheritance – mission accomplished.

Sprinkling our Magic: What wizard companies do.

Stakeholder: Heartless vampire sucking your business dry.

Succession Planning: Preventing them from nicking your job.

Strategic Staircase: Only use when the elevator pitch doesn't work.

Swallow the frog: You won't eat it if you look at it too long – as in low hanging fruit.

T

Think outside the box: Still alive then?

Time Management: How to get a Rolex out of business expenses.

Touch Base: Finger in the pie.

U

Unknown unknowns: Things we don't know that we don't know.

User-Friendly: When we find a friend who can use it, we'll let you know.

USP: Unique Soculitherz People – to die for. (A Soculitherz original)

V

Visionate: The Insightful Power of Powerful Insight – can only really be understood by attending an Ant Cracie workshop. (A Soculitherz original)

W

We'd better not let the grass grow: Hurry up.

Window of Opportunity: Only escape through this window in an emergency. It's likely to drop you onto the tracks of your tears.

Wrongside the demographic: Women and men are different

FREEDOM from BOSSES FOREVER

110% commitment: The most support you'll get from someone not good at maths.

120% commitment: Serious brown nosing.

360 degree thinking: What goes round comes around.

www.ingramcontent.com/pod-product-compliance
Lightning Source LLC
Chambersburg PA
CBHW070118110526
44587CB00014BA/2110